Still Searching for Satoshi

Unveiling the Blockchain Revolution

T0225954

Anders Lisdorf

Apress®

Still Searching for Satoshi: Unveiling the Blockchain Revolution

Anders Lisdorf
Lisdorf Consulting, København SV, Denmark

ISBN-13 (pbk): 978-1-4842-9638-7
https://doi.org/10.1007/978-1-4842-9639-4

ISBN-13 (electronic): 978-1-4842-9639-4

Managing Director, Apress Media LLC: Welmoed Spahr
Acquisitions Editor: Susan McDermott
Development Editor: James Markham
Coordinating Editor: Jessica Vakili

Distributed to the book trade worldwide by Springer Science+Business Media New York, 233 Spring Street, 6th Floor, New York, NY 10013. Phone 1-800-SPRINGER, fax (201) 348-4505, e-mail orders-ny@springer-sbm.com, or visit www.springeronline.com. Apress Media, LLC is a California LLC and the sole member (owner) is Springer Science + Business Media Finance Inc (SSBM Finance Inc). SSBM Finance Inc is a **Delaware** corporation.

For information on translations, please e-mail booktranslations@springernature.com; for reprint, paperback, or audio rights, please e-mail bookpermissions@springernature.com.

Apress titles may be purchased in bulk for academic, corporate, or promotional use. eBook versions and licenses are also available for most titles. For more information, reference our Print and eBook Bulk Sales web page at http://www.apress.com/bulk-sales.

Any source code or other supplementary material referenced by the author in this book is available to readers on the Github repository: https://github.com/Apress/Still-Searching-for-Satoshi. For more detailed information, please visit https://www.apress.com/gp/services/source-code.

Paper in this product is recyclable

Table of Contents

About the Author

Although originally trained as a classical scholar with a PhD in Roman history, **Anders Lisdorf** has been working in the tech industry for decades, bringing innovative technologies forth to solve real-world problems. With an experience across many different industries, public as well as private, he has a wide interest in how we can make use of technology and data to improve the lives of everyone. As an entrepreneur he has started multiple tech companies, and as an enterprise architect, he has been responsible for modernization and development of the data services of the city of New York. Anders is the author of *Cloud Computing Basics* and *Demystifying Smart Cities* (Apress).

About the Technical Reviewer

Dr. Tej Anand is an award-winning business technology strategist, consultant, and innovator with a passion for conceiving and successfully implementing transformative data-driven business initiatives. He's known for being a charismatic leader who effectively collaborates across silos to create committed and impactful cross-functional teams. As a published author, adjunct professor, and educator, Dr. Anand also holds multiple patents in healthcare business processes and business intelligence.

Preface

I first paid serious attention to Bitcoin and the blockchain sometime in 2015. I was designing anti-money laundering systems in the financial sector then and immediately saw that Bitcoin would be pretty convenient for this since all transactions were already out there in the open. Admittedly this was probably not the first thought of the majority of Bitcoin enthusiasts. After reading up on it, I saw great potential and started dabbling by buying a small portion of Bitcoin to try it. I also purchased a more significant amount of what I believe to be the first Exchange Traded Fund (ETF) that allowed retail investors to be exposed to Bitcoin. After a short while, some negative stories about Bitcoin emerged. Something about a key developer of the open source development team leaving. I don't remember the details. People were saying that it is all falling apart now. Knowing full well that this thing was one of the investments in my portfolio that could genuinely have a significant nonzero chance of going to zero and coupled with the knowledge that Bitcoin had already appreciated with more than 100% since last year (and consequently probably had only limited upside, right?), I did what many people owning Bitcoin both before and after had done; I believe the technical term for this is "freaked out" and sold it all. Little did I know at the time that scare stories about the imminent collapse of Bitcoin were about as common as a rainy day in my native Denmark.

A few years later, I found myself living in the United States while another boom in Bitcoin was taking place. I suddenly recalled that I had forgotten to sell my initial test purchase of Bitcoin when it was around $800. Now it was all over the news, and even New York Subway info screens, that bitcoin would soon hit the $20,000 mark. I decided this was lunacy, and bitcoin would probably never go higher, so I found my old wallet and cashed out. I used the funds to buy my wife a diamond ring, a good return for a small technological experiment. I wish there were more of these.

After that, my assessment of Bitcoin soured, and I thought it had degraded into a Ponzi scheme that never really seriously tried to fulfill its potential for good. Sometimes I would make critical comments about Bitcoin on Quora or Twitter only to be flooded with trolls ridiculing me and telling me how big an idiot I was. So naturally, I lost interest.

Today I can look back and note that had I not freaked out and held my initial investment in the Bitcoin ETF, I would actually have been able to buy the Lamborghini that is so coveted in the Bitcoin community. My story is not uncommon for many regular people, or normies as they are called in the Bitcoin community. Some have been lucky to hit the jackpot and get rich. Most have not.

As I am writing this, the crypto market has fallen back down. I do not own Bitcoin either directly or indirectly. I have run through the full spectrum of enthusiasm, disdain, and indifference toward Bitcoin. However, I still feel that this is such a fascinating and unique technological development that it needs to have its story told neutrally and objectively. There is no shortage of books on Bitcoin or experts willing to tell you all about it. The problem is that they are invariably heavily invested in it and consequently heavily invested in portraying it positively. That does not mean there are no critics, but they stand completely outside. They have typically decided early on that Bitcoin was a scam and not found it necessary to study it more than superficially. This leaves a gaping hole for the curious and open nontechnical readers who just want to understand what all the fuss is about and be able to make up their own minds about this Bitcoin and blockchain thing.

Bitcoin is currently under heavy headwinds in terms of regulatory pressure and scandals, but even if you think Bitcoin has peaked, it is still such a remarkable technological achievement, unlike anything the modern world has produced, that it warrants serious attention.

If you are not already hooked on Bitcoin but are curious about what it is and what it could be, this book is for you. I hope to be able to guide you through the fascinating thoughts and history behind Bitcoin and the blockchain, to illuminate the aspects of human civilization that Bitcoin addresses as well as provide a view into the future of what the blockchain might become. Even if you are already hooked on Bitcoin, I hope you will be able to find new pieces of information and perspectives. It has been my intention to give a balanced account that does not dismiss Bitcoin out of hand nor latch on to the most excessive claims about its wonders.

Introduction

One Satoshi Nakamoto first announced Bitcoin on October 13, 2008. It is the first implementation of a cryptocurrency on what is called the blockchain, and as such, it is ground zero for the blockchain revolution and the technologies that flow from it, like smart contracts, cryptocurrencies, NFTs, DAOs, and the so-called Web3, to name a few. These new and exotic phenomena purport to disrupt payment and transcend the way we do business and the existing global order. One will be forgiven for a touch of skepticism at the magnitude and rate with which our world is supposed to change, according to cryptocurrency advocates. Still, even to the casual observer, it seems reasonable to assume that we can at least expect some significant change due to the blockchain revolution.

There is plenty of material to read up on Bitcoin and the blockchain. Today there are multiple excellent books on the subject by accomplished writers and Bitcoin specialists. Pundits always appear ready to explain and comment on podcasts, radio, and TV.

Unfortunately, with few exceptions, treatments of Bitcoin and the blockchain fall into one of two groups. The first group is the advocates, who think Bitcoin and the blockchain will solve all problems the world has faced and, in due time, create a utopia with equal and fair distribution of wealth, the end of war, and the ability for everyone to do anything they want. The second group is the critics, who are just as convinced that it is all just a fad that will collapse in a glorious implosion. To this group, Bitcoin is nothing more than a Ponzi scheme used by pump-and-dump speculators to enrich themselves.

This polarization is reflected in the discourse about Bitcoin. The experts and pundits are invariably advocates, who are themselves deeply invested in Bitcoin and cryptocurrencies and consequently stand to gain personally the more popular Bitcoin becomes as an investment object. There are clear disclosure rules when discussing securities in the regulated financial industry that Bitcoin seeks to compete with regarding deal flow. In most cases, analysts are even barred from investing in the securities they cover. This starkly contrasts the Bitcoin analysts and pundits that appear in the media. The neutral observer is consequently left speculating how much of the analysis about Bitcoin and the blockchain is motivated by personal gain and how much is impartial analysis. Investing in something you know a lot about and believe strongly in is not necessarily anything weird or wrong. But it is problematic when you also appear in public as an expert and advocate for it.

Critics often dismiss Bitcoin and the blockchain. If you listen to this group, you may well have a similar problem since they are typically embedded in the status quo of the financial system. They are frequently representatives of the banking system that Bitcoin and cryptocurrencies are disrupting or investment advisers that specialize in traditional forms of investment. It is also unconvincing to the neutral observer.

We are therefore left with a situation where it is hard to find neutral and impartial information about Bitcoin and the blockchain. I am uniquely positioned to offer such an unbiased perspective since I am not directly or indirectly invested in bitcoin or other cryptocurrencies. I consequently have nothing to gain personally from either the success or failure of Bitcoin, cryptocurrencies, or the blockchain.

In this book, we will not fall into any of the extremes and look at the phenomenon critically but with curiosity. Even if Bitcoin turns out to be a scam and all other blockchains collapse, it is already clear that it has stirred deep emotions and pointed to weak points in the financial system that need to be addressed. This fact alone warrants a thorough treatment of a phenomenon that has captivated a large part of the technological and financial world for over a decade.

What Is Bitcoin?

At the outset of this book, a reasonable question might be, "What is Bitcoin?" This seems innocent and straightforward enough, but the simplicity of the question is deceptive. A first observation is related to the precision of language. The word *Bitcoin* with a capital B is usually used for the Bitcoin technology in general, while *bitcoin* is for the currency. If the answer were straightforward, there would not be a plethora of books, courses, and short introductions on different media on the Internet. There would not be endless memes with people trying to explain Bitcoin. Unlike everyday objects like coffee, cars, or bananas, there isn't anything we can point to as a reference.

That may not be surprising since Bitcoin is a virtual thing without any physical appearance to point to. But unlike other virtual things like Facebook or Google Search, we still can't point to any one thing that comprehensively describes what Bitcoin is. Facebook, for example, is a site that you log into, which connects you with your friends. You can see what they are up to, what events they are attending, and when is their birthday. It blends seamlessly into our social lives as just another way to do regular social activities. While it has made communication easier, it does not fundamentally challenge any fundamental practice or concepts we had from the outset. Google Search is similarly a massive improvement in how we find information, the scale of which has never been seen before. Still, it solves a basic problem that humans have faced since the invention of writing and libraries: how to index, find, and retrieve discrete pieces of information. We can intuitively relate to this when we go to our bookshelf to retrieve the *Wisden Cricketers' Almanack* to see how many test match runs Kevin Pietersen scored in his career. For those who do not have physical books, a walk through any large retailer to find any product, say a coffee grinder, presents much the same problem. The information is indexed by sections with different themes (you are looking for cooking items). If you can't find it, you can ask that friendly and ubiquitous store clerk who will inform you that it is in Isle 17. For those who can't relate to this experience either because everything you do is online, you should just know that all the search you do on your devices has been developed by previous generations' intuitions about how to retrieve information.

Bitcoin is different. You don't log into Bitcoin to do anything in particular. Sure, you can use it for payment in some circumstances. But here, it starts to diverge from our usual experience. To use it for payment, you need a so-called wallet. For cash, a wallet is nice enough to have but not necessary. I can also put my credit cards in my pocket without any wallet. Our everyday experience has a wallet as an incidental aspect of payment, whereas for Bitcoin it is necessary. We are not talking about a physical wallet though. Indeed our day-to-day experience of payment depends to some degree on a physical aspect, like notes, coins, and cards, not a virtual digital construct that requires a long and complicated "password" for identification and retrieval of contents of the wallet. Furthermore, the Bitcoin wallet is not issued by any institution, even if it might be mediated by one, such as Coinbase. There is no recourse if anything related to the transaction fails. No hotline, no customer service, no way to complain.

Moreover, Bitcoin is also considered an investment, a so-called store of value, like gold or platinum, which you can buy as an Exchange Traded Fund (ETF). In this case, you do not own bitcoin yourself, but it is owned through an institution. So far, it may still be somewhat intuitive since it is possible to invest in currency with your local bank. Now is where it gets weird because Bitcoin can also be used as a way to document contracts. Oh, and also, you can make bitcoin yourself by mining, something absolutely not advisable for other forms of currency used for payment.

If you want, you can also see all other transactions ever made in bitcoin since its inception. Slowly our everyday concepts of familiar things are starting to break down: is this a currency, a store of value, a certification engine, or a computational job agency?

The answer is that Bitcoin is all of these and more. We are therefore challenged to find other ways than our ordinary experience to characterize Bitcoin as a phenomenon.

Bitcoin As a Cosmogram

In his book *Digital Cash*, Finn Brunton presents an exciting view of digital currencies in general and Bitcoin in particular. Following the historian of technology John Tresch, he sees digital currencies as cosmograms. Cosmograms are things that order our cosmos and our place in it. They embed a system of relationships, actions, and roles that define a cosmos in a concentrated fashion. The cosmogram thus becomes "(...) a model of the world with an agenda, an implicit utopian project expressed through an arrangement of objects and symbols." Examples include Buddhist mandalas that depict the cosmos in the shape of a square pattern with different patterns and figures. One features the five Buddhas that embody various aspects of enlightenment. As such, they refer to a practice of meditation, reading of mantras, and a body of wisdom and ethical practice, all imprinted in the cosmogram.

Bitcoin also embodies a model of the cosmos, albeit a more limited one related to the ideal nature of financial transactions and monetary systems, but also, as we shall see, the individuals' relation with the government and economic policy. In this cosmogram, there is no central authority, only individual participants (miners and wallet users) that define the nature of reality (the transactions that are considered real) through a process of consensus. It offers an image of the world as it could be with no interference from the government and a currency where no individual decides whether to print more money. The rate of money supply is already given (until around the year 2140 where it will cease) in the cosmographical imprint that is the Bitcoin source code. The cosmographical imprint, like the Buddhist mandalas, also produces and organizes the world. For example, it organizes time into blocks of transactions approximately every ten minutes. In this world, anyone is free to join. No central authority like a bank needs to vet you and grant you a bank account. A world of financial egalitarianism secured by cryptographic certainty guardrails the privacy of the individual and what they might choose to spend their money on. There is no surveillance by a big brother and no need for trust.

Bitcoin As a Heterotopia

Bitcoin is not just a model but also constitutes a kind of place. French philosopher Michel Foucault suggested that a unique kind of place exists, one that is not quite like the utopia, which is fundamentally unreal, but a real place that points to other spaces in a special way. He calls this a heterotopia after the Greek *heteros*, meaning "different," and *topos*, meaning "place." A heterotopia is thus a somehow different space.

Utopias are idealizations of society that, by their nature, do not exist and are not real. They are defined by tension with the real. Heterotopias, on the contrary, are real places that reach out of the present place and define other possibilities. An example of a heterotopia is a zoo; it is a real place but one that relates to other real spaces where the different animals come from.

Another example is the amusement park that in itself is radically different from the surroundings. In the amusement park, you lose the sense of the place around you and are transported to another world of fun and imagination. These heterotopias are unique places with special functions, aesthetics, and possibilities. In a sense, Bitcoin can be seen as one such virtual heterotopia.

According to Foucault, they exhibit some fundamental properties. They can, in a single space, juxtapose other real spaces that are in themselves incompatible. The traditional Persian garden was supposed to bring together the four corners of the world in a microcosm, where the garden is the smallest parcel of the world but also represents the whole world. A contemporary version of this is the zoo, where different incompatible ecosystems and climate zones are juxtaposed in the same space. Bitcoin and the blockchain also do this since it is at once the private space of everyone there but also at the same time a completely public space since everything is out in the open. Bitcoin thus juxtaposes complete privacy with radical publicness.

Heterotopias also typically have a peculiar relationship with time. They constitute a break with traditional time, such as can be seen in a museum or library that contains indefinitely accumulating time. Prehistory meets antiquity and medieval times in the same space. Foucault calls this property heterochrony. The cemetery is also such a place where the past accumulates in the present. In the blockchain, this is seen in the fact that all past transactions are always present. Indeed the beating heart of the blockchain, the formation of a new block, defines the present through a relation to all of the past blocks in the blockchain as Chronos devouring his children.

Heterotopias are also interesting because they define an "other space," a real but perfect space, as opposed to the messy and ill-formed character of the normal space around it. An example is colonies like the Puritan societies of the English in America or the Jesuits of Paraguay. These colonies defined the perfect space in contrast to the mundane space that was left behind in the old world. In much the same way, the blockchain represents an ideal system with no middlemen and no trust in anyone, where transactions can flow freely. Like the Puritan ideals were enacted in a real space in contrast to the world left behind, the ideals embedded in Bitcoin and the blockchain create a space of tension toward the old world that is left behind.

Bitcoin and the blockchain could thus be said to constitute a virtual heterotopia. Had it just been another whitepaper or sci-fi novel, it would have been merely a utopia, but its implementation as a real space in the world shifted it to a heterotopia with specific new properties and possibilities.

Bitcoin As a Hyperobject

In a way, Bitcoin can also be said to transcend not just time but also space. Philosopher Timothy Bloxam Morton has introduced the hyperobject concept to characterize non-local entities in space and time. Examples include global warming, oil reserves, or the English language; you can't quite grasp the entirety of the hyperobject even if you do perceive it. You can experience rain or forest fires, but that does not constitute climate change. Climate change as a hyperobject interacts with the real world in weather phenomena and measurements, but because of its immensity can't be reduced to such interactions.

Hyperobjects exhibit a few characteristics that differentiate them from normal objects humans can perceive. They are non-local with regard to time and space. From this perspective, oil reserves are not just the black oily goo captured in the ground but also the plants and animals that produced the organic chemical compounds from which the oil derives. As such, the timescale becomes one of millennia, where the past intersects with the present in the physical appearance as the gasoline that allows me to drive my car from one place to the next. In the same way, Bitcoin depends on the past since the coins were generated, and any balance to be used by any person in a transaction depends on the generation of past bitcoins. But it is also nontrivially affected by the future since it is built into Bitcoin that the supply is finite and will stop at some point in the future. This property creates the deflationary forces of bitcoin; the scarcity and hence the contemporary value are produced by Bitcoin in the future.

Bitcoin is also radically non-local in a geographical sense since it is the product of a distributed system, a mesh of processing nodes that mine bitcoin. These nodes can join and leave the Bitcoin processing network from anywhere in time and space. The Bitcoin hyperobject affects these local physical machines in non-local ways since it depends on a distributed ledger that is shared and produced by this mesh irrespective of any particular physical device.

Hyperobjects also have the property of being phased; they have a higher-dimensional phase space that is impossible to perceive directly. To imagine the intelligibility of higher-dimensional processes, imagine a two-dimensional creature living in a world that resembles a piece of paper. This two-dimensional creature would only be able to perceive lines and dots in the plane of its two-dimensional world. Now imagine a three-dimensional ball passing through. To our two-dimensional creature, this would appear as a dot that expanded to a line, which then contracted into a dot and disappeared.

A phase space is all the possible configurations of a system. Every parameter is presented as a dimension in a multidimensional space. A two-dimensional system is called a phase plane. The system's evolution traces a path over time that can be recorded in a phase plane. But this trajectory is defined by processes and forces that operate in a multidimensional space. Much as the ball's appearance to the two-dimensional creature, the trajectory over time will be understood only by an understanding of the initial conditions and forces operating in all the dimensions, that is, everything from the initial configuration of all parameters of the system to the forces affecting the system in each dimension. Such dimensions might for Bitcoin include the hash rate (the total CPU power working on the network), the supply of bitcoin, the transaction volume, etc. The effects of the hyperobject Bitcoin in this multidimensional space can be traced to the price of bitcoin. The volatility, the booms, and the bust cycles, if you will, are the effects of processes in the multidimensional phase space.

The last property of hyperobjects to consider is that they are inter-objective. The English language, for example, depends on books written, words spoken, and other languages. This forms a mesh of objects that interact with each other. We find French words in English and English words in French. The language also evolves through interaction, which we see in how it is written in tweets, videos, and texts; new words appear here that do not appear in the historical books, stretching the meanings and contents of the English language as a whole. This is a mesh of relations between objects. The same dynamic can be seen for Bitcoin, where bitcoin is used as a bridge to other cryptocurrencies: in order to buy other cryptocurrencies, you typically need to go through bitcoin to exchange it in cryptocurrency crosses. It is therefore affected by the popularity and use of such cryptocurrencies. Likewise, bitcoin is also used as a currency cross with regular fiat currencies and is affected by processes in the world of traditional finance, as can be seen by how economic crises drive the price of bitcoin up or down.

Starting the Search

Whatever Bitcoin is, it is not straightforward to grasp. There are multiple ways of understanding it; we have not arrived upon the one true understanding yet. Just like the identity of the inventor, Satoshi Nakamoto, continues to elude us, the true nature and constitution of Bitcoin similarly elude us. This is why in a literal and metaphorical way, we can see that we are still searching for Satoshi, as the title of this book suggests. It is to this literal and figurative search for Satoshi and the nature of Bitcoin and the blockchain that we will devote the rest of this book to clarify.

Outline of the Book

The first part of the book is a technological history, which reviews the key developments that Bitcoin builds on. These developed more or less independently and combined into Bitcoin. Once they are explained, it is possible to give a deeper explanation of how Bitcoin works. This understanding will inform the remaining parts of the book.

We will look at the history of electronic or virtual money before Bitcoin. The dream of having to dispense with the physical aspects of money is an old one, and several unsuccessful attempts had been made before Bitcoin. By eliminating the physical aspects of money, forgery is impossible or at least transformed into an electronic effort. But with that come new problems and regulatory challenges.

Critical developments in cryptography in the twentieth century paved the way for Bitcoin. The purpose of cryptography is to keep information private by preserving its confidentiality and integrity. Cryptography has a long history and has only recently developed into a dedicated academic field. The advent of the electronic computer only exacerbated already existing trends, which led to the development of new techniques designed to mitigate the connected world of the Internet and resulted in fundamentally new approaches to millennia-old problems.

Based on the knowledge we gained about the historical antecedents, we will piece together how Bitcoin and the blockchain work. We will see how central concepts like wallet, blockchain, mining, and the Bitcoin token work in the Bitcoin system to provide a global virtual currency.

After the general historical investigation, we will turn our attention to the particular historical aspects surrounding the emergence of Bitcoin. We will try to provide a historical account of the development and look at what the sources can tell us about the mysterious inventor: Satoshi Nakamoto.

We will try to provide some insight into who the historical Satoshi Nakamoto is. Much previous writing about Bitcoin has focused on who the historical person or persons behind Satoshi Nakamoto were, but we will apply a historical critical perspective to this question and sift through the available evidence to create a better understanding of what we can and cannot say about the identity of Satoshi Nakamoto.

Since 2011 much investigation and speculation has been done by established journalists and amateur bloggers alike. But what do the sources actually say? By focusing on the sources, we are able to extract several key characteristics to look for. This will allow us to build a profile of Satoshi. From the basis of the primary sources, we will constitute a list of possible historical persons who could be Satoshi and match them to the profile. Indeed we will find that there is one and only one clear match.

The last part of the book will try to put Bitcoin in context and look at how Bitcoin can be viewed in the broader context of human civilization since it does not exist in a technological vacuum addressing only technological issues but is rather firmly situated in a web of themes that are and have been central to human civilization.

Since prehistoric times humans have engaged in exchange. This has taken many different shapes on a continuum from barter, through intermediaries such as cowry shells, gold, and silver coins, to purely symbolic means of exchange. We will look at the history and nature of money and see how Bitcoin fits.

Social organization is critical to understanding cultural phenomena. We will consequently look deeper into the different types of social organizations that have been associated with Bitcoin. We will look at the cypherpunks, libertarians, and open source development communities and how the nature and vision of Bitcoin are tied to the social organization in which it developed and is used.

A rarely debated issue is the religious aspects of Bitcoin and the crypto movement. But these aspects are nothing new when it comes to human cultures. Understanding this helps explain many of Bitcoin believers' seemingly strange behavior without claiming that Bitcoin is an actual religion. We can see definite resemblances in the prophet, Satoshi Nakamoto; the sacred scriptures, the Bitcoin whitepaper; the classification of true believers and heathens; and the ubiquitous millenarianist aspects.

We will then look at the possible future of Bitcoin. Based on a few future development scenarios, we will reason about how Bitcoin might fit. Based on the insights we have gathered over the course of the book, we can hypothetically model how Bitcoin might develop in different circumstances.

In the final chapter, we will go beyond the human perspective and try to look at Bitcoin from a different perspective. We will ask the question of whether Bitcoin might be alive by comparing it with the criteria of ordinary biological life. We will find that, surprisingly, it is an independent hyperorganism that shows signs of being alive.

CHAPTER 1

Virtual Currency

The dream of dispensing with the physical aspects of money is old. Several attempts had been made before Bitcoin. Throughout human history, an incredible array of mediums have been used as money ranging from massive stones on the Yap Islands, over seashells in Melanesia, to paper notes in China. The diversity and imaginative thrust notwithstanding, money always had a physical aspect.

The physicality of money has apparent drawbacks. If one needed to go to the market in the next town to buy a horse, it was necessary to bring the money for that. This limits what mediums can be used as money since the weight would have to be carried or otherwise transported. Bricks and trunks of wood were thus not good choices for money. More common were smaller rare objects like seashells, beads, and precious metals, while in more recent history, paper notes gained popularity too. These provided a tolerable solution for the problem of transportation. Still, the money had to be stored between exchange events, which meant that it could be destroyed in the event of a fire, corroded in the case of metals like silver and copper, or crushed in the case of shells. The physical world allows for many possible ways of destruction, which is unfortunate. A further problem is the risk of theft since ownership of money can only be determined by possession. Add to these woes the possibility of forgery, whereby new money is produced and illicitly introduced into the economy.

© Anders Lisdorf 2023
A. Lisdorf, *Still Searching for Satoshi*, https://doi.org/10.1007/978-1-4842-9639-4_1

There are consequently many good reasons to wish for a virtual currency whereby these physical adversities would disappear. Some of these issues were eliminated by introducing checks and credit cards in the twentieth century. But these new technologies, in turn, introduced new problems. Checks have to be cleared and can bounce, so a transaction is not necessarily final at the time the check is written. The same is the case for credit cards. Payments take days to clear and can be contested subsequently. These were never issues with physical money. Another grief some people have is that banks are necessary intermediaries with a privileged view into our private lives that they should not have due to the fundamental right to privacy. Again, something different from physical money. A virtual currency is consequently not just a virtually mediated way of spending regular physical money; it is a new way to support exchange of goods and services that brings its own unique possibilities and challenges.

What Is a Virtual Currency?

The definition of *virtual currency* is contested. Most can agree that virtual currency does not need a physical manifestation, but can it have a physical manifestation? If yes, how? Even among regulators, there has yet to be a consensus on different aspects in the European Union (EU) and United States.

The term *virtual currency* has been used in different contexts throughout the twentieth century. It can be documented back to the start of the previous century in the context of monetary theory. It was used in the sense of something in place of a currency. As such, it was used, for example, to describe how Spanish colonies in the eighteenth and nineteenth centuries used notes as money. It has also been used concerning the so-called prediction markets that gained popularity toward the end of the twentieth century. Here one could bet on a prediction of an event with a virtual currency and win if it came true. The virtual currency could have an exchange rate for real currency.

Around the turn of the millennium, the euro was initially used before the European Central Bank (ECB) started to issue notes and coins. This was described as a virtual currency. It was also used in more popular circles in the 2000s, where the currency of the online game *Second Life*, called Linden dollars, was described as a virtual currency.

The term *virtual currency* can therefore be seen to have a story that predates Bitcoin and other cryptocurrencies. However, it was only after Bitcoin emerged that regulators felt compelled to define virtual currencies formally.

In October 2012, the European Central Bank published a report on cryptocurrency schemes. This was motivated by the observation that virtual communities started circulating their own currencies. Given that the ECB is the central authority of the European banking system providing oversight of payments, they felt the need to clarify this phenomenon. The ECB defined *virtual currency* as "(...) as a type of unregulated, digital money, which is issued and usually controlled by its developers, and used and accepted among the members of a specific virtual community." They note that it differs from electronic money because it has no physical counterpart with legal tender status.

Virtual currencies are thus not the money you transfer through your online banking system or credit card payments even though this might be experienced as a virtual transfer of funds. These are digitally mediated currency transactions. Virtual currencies are, according to the ECB, currencies that are issued by private entities. In the report, they distinguish three types. Type 1 is closed virtual currency schemes as used internally in online games. Here, the currency is generated inside the virtual entity and is not officially exchanged with real currency. By real currency, we mean currency that has legal tender somewhere. Type 2 has a unidirectional flow where it is possible to purchase the virtual currency that can be used for virtual goods and services and sometimes for physical goods and services. This type is also prevalent in online games. Type 3 has a bidirectional flow and acts like any other convertible currency with a buy-and-sell rate.

These can be used to purchase real or virtual goods and services. Bitcoin and other cryptocurrencies fall into this type; they can be exchanged online and used for payments.

This was merely an initial assessment of the new phenomenon of virtual currencies by one EU body. In 2018 came a more comprehensive directive that set the legal parameters of virtual currencies for the EU in relation to money laundering and financial crime. This directive is an amendment to the Directive 2015/849, the purpose of which is to prevent the use of the financial system for money laundering and financing of terrorism.

Here *virtual currency* is defined as "(…) a digital representation of value that is not issued or guaranteed by a central bank or a public authority, is not necessarily attached to a legally established currency, and does not possess a legal status of currency or money, but is accepted by natural or legal persons as a means of exchange and which can be transferred, stored and traded electronically" (p. 54).

In the United States, the Department of the Treasury Financial Crimes Enforcement Network (FinCEN) took upon itself to issue guidance clarifying its views on virtual currencies in 2013. According to FinCEN, a virtual currency is viewed in contrast to real currencies and is consequently seen as "a medium of exchange that operates like a currency in some environments but does not have all the attributes of real currency. In particular, virtual currency does not have legal tender status in any jurisdiction."

FinCEN was primarily concerned with the different activities related to virtual currencies and distinguished three types of agents and their obligations. These are "users," "administrators," and "exchangers". Users are not considered money transmitters, but administrators and exchangers are. Similarly to the European Union, virtual currencies were initially approached from a crime prevention perspective. Still, soon after followed other regulatory bodies like the Internal Revenue Service (IRS) and the US Commodity Futures Trading Commission (CFTC) that have determined that virtual currencies are to be considered property and a commodity, respectively, not currency.

This ruling came to have a significant impact on the trajectory of Bitcoin, which until then had been in regulatory limbo. To some, it was interpreted as a hindrance to the free development of the virtual currency. To others, it was positive since it did not criminalize virtual currencies altogether. Ordinary people would continue to be allowed to use cryptocurrencies.

In summary, there seems to be a consensus that virtual currencies have the following properties:

1. Digital representation of value

2. Issued by a private or non-government entity

3. Used as a means of exchange

Furthermore, three types of virtual currency can be distinguished:

> Type 1 (internal): Digital value is generated and exchanged within a closed virtual community.

> Type 2 (unidirectional): Virtual currency can be bought with real currency and spent.

> Type 3 (bidirectional): Virtual currency can be bought and sold.

We will concern ourselves mainly with type 3 virtual currencies, where regular currency can be converted back and forth between the virtual currency.

The Dream of a Virtual Currency

Even long before the first virtual currencies were implemented, dreams and visions described what they could be. Some of those ideas were surprisingly close to the end products that took shape around the turn of the new millennium. These ideas inspired and helped shape the first attempts at virtual currencies. We will need to review these early visions to fully appreciate the later trajectory of virtual currencies.

The Austrian economist Friedrich Hayek was and is a major inspiration for much of the cryptocurrency world. A Nobel laureate, he was one of the major figures of the Austrian School of Economy. One of his theses was that money should be taken out of the grasp of the state and, instead, several private currencies should be allowed to compete freely. It is easy to see why this would inspire Bitcoin and other virtual currencies. Hayek's vision of money was one where spontaneous order would arise not out of human planning, as the nation-state model of currency has it, but out of human action in a free market of currencies. Thus, a collective brain would arise out of multiple non-governmental currencies. Only the digital representation aspect of virtual currencies is missing from Hayek's conception of virtual currency. The rest is already there to be picked up by later generations.

The technologies for an actual virtual currency were absent when Hayek was writing his major works. However, with the advent of the modern personal computer in the 1980s and the general availability of the Internet in the 1990s, a digital representation of value became possible or at least imaginable. For the first generation of hackers, the baby boomers, and the counter-culture-inspired computer programmers, ideas of liberty and freedom ranked high. The dream was not just for software and information to be free but also for the use of money to be free.

In the world of science fiction, ideas about the future that still guide us today were shaped. One of the most influential early pieces of science fiction was the 1981 novella *True Names* by Vernor Vinge, a San Diego–based mathematics professor. In *True Names*, Vinge presents a vision of a world mediated by computers called "Other Plane," perhaps the first to portray a vision of a parallel virtual world that William Gibson would later adopt in his novel *Neuromancer* where the term "cyberspace" was used and Neal Stephenson would adopt in *Snow Crash*, where the term "metaverse" was coined. In *True Names*, we follow a group of hackers whose names are secret even to each other. They venture into the "Other Plane" to break into computers to steal information. They must keep their names confidential so the government does not catch them. This novel introduced the concept of a virtual world where privacy was necessary to hide from the government. But in Vinge's world, there is no virtual currency. Banks and currency continue to exist.

Vinge's vision was picked up by Timothy C. May. May was an engineer who had retired at 34 from Intel after calculating how much he would need to remain independent for the rest of his life. May was a founding member of the cypherpunk movement, out of which Bitcoin would grow, and was the author of *The Crypto Anarchist Manifesto*, which also came to be a driving inspiration in the quest for a private virtual currency.

In 1993 he wrote a piece of fiction that built on the world created by Vinge in which an organization called BlackNet was dealing in a black market of information. None of the members of BlackNet knew each other's true names. One could communicate with this group through public online newsgroups (forums). BlackNet would post a public key with which to encrypt the message. To write to them, you could use this public key together with a private key to create a message that only BlackNet could decrypt. The message contained the requested information and payment terms. It was possible for BlackNet to make anonymous deposits to your bank account or, more interestingly, to credit you in "CryptoCredits," the internal currency of BlackNet. CryptoCredits could be saved and spent on other secret information. In this fictitious world that is built on known technologies, we see the contours of future cryptocurrencies almost 20 years before any such was created.

Anonymous Digital Cash Awakens

The story of David Chaum and his company DigiCash and the rise of its product eCash is one of a pioneer, years if not decades ahead of his time. But it was also one that influenced Bitcoin and all subsequent virtual currencies due to its successful implementation and relative early success. For many, this became a beacon for what a virtual currency had to be as a minimum.

Already in the 1980s, David Chaum was working on the idea of digital cash. In his 1982 paper "Blind signatures for untraceable payments," he took issue with the lack of privacy inherent in electronic payments. Through payment information, quite a deal of private information could be gathered about the payee. This was a theme that would recur in subsequent discussions about virtual currencies. The proposition was to eliminate this with the use of cryptography. The paper is merely an outline of the idea rather than an actual system. Through the use of so-called blind signatures achieved with cryptographic techniques, it would be possible to provide a payment system that would make payments untraceable but auditable to verify that the transaction had indeed taken place. This system does not speak of a new and separate currency but instead provides a way for the existing banking and payment systems to work in a confidential manner.

In 1990 Chaum founded a company based on this idea called DigiCash. DigiCash created the first functional private digital payment system. The system allowed people to move money from their bank account to DigiCash's eCash. With this eCash, you could pay merchants accepting it as you would with a credit card. The difference was that the payment would only verify that you had the funds and the merchants could redeem it at the issuing bank. All of this without anyone knowing the identity of the person who made the transaction. The process was as follows: When you want to pay, you withdraw money from your bank like an ATM. The bank generates a note for the amount with a serial number. Using cryptography, it is possible to create a serial number that does not lead back to the user but certifies that it is a real note backed by real money. In this system, the identity of the merchant was not anonymous. In this way, DigiCash created a system that secured the user's privacy without aiding criminals in staying hidden. Incidentally, this may be why DigiCash's eCash is the only implemented example of a virtual currency that did not have issues with criminal abuse and money laundering allegations.

DigiCash was relatively successful, and its software existed for all standard operating systems; deals were being negotiated with Visa, ING, and Deutsche Bank. Microsoft even offered to buy it to integrate it into the Windows operating system, but within a decade DigiCash was bankrupt. This was probably more due to the failures on the management side than any technological, regulatory, or market causes. Still, the legacy can't be underestimated as it provided a reference point and proof that a private digital cash was feasible, inspiring subsequent attempts at digital currencies. The focus was squarely on the consumer's privacy, not evading the government or creating a new currency of speculative relevance. Other projects supplied these objectives.

The Liberation of the Dollar

After DigiCash, another attempt was made at creating a currency in the form of the Liberty dollar. Although it also had a virtual component, its conception came from a physical manifestation in the shape of a silver dollar. It was fueled by the very same ideas as other virtual currencies, and its demise illuminated a theme that would come to dominate digital currencies in decades to follow.

Bernard von NotHaus had long speculated about value. Already in 1974, he and his partner Telle Presley wrote an essay titled "To Know Value—An Economic Research Paper." This document referencing Aldous Huxley and Swami Kriyananda argued that only gold is real and should be the basis of value. This strikes another cord that we will repeatedly see among libertarians and Bitcoin enthusiasts: the regret of losing the gold standard leading to the continuous printing of money by central banks, leading to inflation. Von NotHaus was adamantly opposed to the Federal Reserve and founded the organization "National Organization for the Repeal of the Federal Reserve" (NORFED).

In 1998 it started to issue silver Liberty dollars through the Sunshine Minting company based in Coeur d'Alene, Idaho. Later gold and platinum versions were also available. These could be bought at the silver, gold, or platinum price. Since it is illegal to make or sell coins of gold or other metals with the intention of use as money in the United States, they were emphatic that they were medallions and not legal tender. The coins could be bought physically but also through a warehouse receipt that could be exchanged for a Liberty dollar at their warehouse in Idaho. While the warehouse receipts were pieces of paper, more interestingly, they could also be issued digitally as eLibertyDollars. The Liberty dollar thus presents a digital store of value, one of the three properties of money, while it was not used as a means of exchange or unit of account, the other two properties.

Unfortunately for Bernard von NotHaus, the United States disagreed that Liberty dollars were mere medallions, and in November 2007 the offices were raided by the FBI and Secret Service who seized all the coins there. Von NotHaus was arrested in 2009 and eventually convicted for making and selling his own coins in 2011. While his appeal was unsuccessful, the sentence was reduced from the 23 years in prison demanded by the prosecutor to six months of house arrest and three years of probation. A significant number of Liberty dollars were subsequently returned to their owners.

While showing that there was indeed a market for alternative coins (more than 250,000 were sold) and that digital representations of stores of value were feasible, the Liberty dollar also provided a cautionary tale for all subsequent alternative currencies. It demonstrated the risk of years of prolonged trials and possible incarceration.

Digital Gold Currencies

This quest for private people to own gold and other precious metals that the Liberty dollar built on was picked up by other similar initiatives. Up through the 1990s and early aughts, there was a spike in companies that offered consumers to buy and sell gold digitally. These are commonly known as digital gold currencies (DGCs). Some were driven by idealists, while others descended into criminal behavior or were downright scams from the beginning. The legal aftermath of one of these companies, e-gold, is the most interesting due to its size and success.

The history of private ownership of gold in the United States is a traumatic one. It is a history that fueled the quest for fair virtual currencies that would funnel into cryptocurrencies. To understand why we need to go back to April 5, 1933, when Harry S. Truman signed Executive Order 6102, which forbade citizens from owning gold in the United States. This was in effect until repealed by Gerald Ford in 1974. Owning gold was still a rather cumbersome affair since one would have to procure it somewhere, transport it, and keep it safe. Holding it was thus a niche affair, but the demand was broader. We have to remember that today it is easy to buy and own gold through an online brokerage, but such were only available to a small number of people around the turn of the century. As mentioned previously, there was a significant niche with a libertarian bent that distrusted government in general and the Federal Reserve and its ability to administrate the issuance of currency in particular. For these people, the fall from grace happened with the abolition of the gold standard in the 1920s, whereby money was pegged to gold. Under the gold standard, converting money to gold at a fixed rate and converting it to other currencies was easy. Since the gold standard could not be re-established, the next best thing was to own gold oneself.

e-gold was founded in 1996 by oncologist Douglas Jackson and attorney Barry Downey. Their purpose was to make it possible for ordinary people to buy and trade gold digitally. All e-gold was backed by actual physical gold. Through their system, it was possible for users to instantly transfer any amount of gold or other precious metals that they had on their account to another account. This was anonymous and final. If a user had transferred the gold to the wrong account, there was nothing that the company could do except relay a request to the user with a request to transfer it back.

e-gold set a new standard for transparency as their possessions were audited and updated daily. The serial numbers of the bullions were published for all to see. The company also did its best to stay compliant, for example, by asking the IRS for an audit to determine what regulations they would have to follow.

While the start was slow, it accelerated after the turn of the century. At its peak, it was processing more than 2 billion USD per year, and it had 5 million accounts when its operations were halted in 2009. While the Liberty dollar was primarily about a store of value and a statement, e-gold had more success as a means of exchange (it was even used as a form of payment on eBay), so much so that it was eventually also used by criminals and money launderers. Finally, Douglas Jackson and Barry Downey ended up being charged with running an unlicensed money-transmitting business and conspiracy to engage in money laundering. Although they tried tenaciously to defend themselves against the charges, they entered a plea agreement that gave the two founders fines, home detention, and community service. The money in accounts was eventually disbursed to clients, and the company closed down. To many people interested in virtual currencies, this was a key case where the founders tried their best to follow regulations but still got criminalized and prosecuted by the government. This reinforced the idea of a government that could not be trusted.

Ecommerce Rises

While these previous efforts at making virtual currencies were primarily driven by libertarian ideology, the dot-com era and commercialization of the Internet provided space for a new type of use for virtual currency. Around the turn of the millennium, the Internet was still very much an information-sharing project. Trading anything was risky and cumbersome. At this time, there was no established payment method, and it was unclear which form would be dominant. The credit card companies and PayPal had yet to win the battle for digital payment. In this context, other options were being considered and tried out.

The time leading up to the dot-com crash of 2000 was a happy one full of optimism for ecommerce. The Internet was turning from an information-sharing platform to a platform for commerce. The only problem was that the Internet was not in any way built for this to be done safely and securely. Information was meant to be open and shared, not secret like you would expect regarding money. This presented merchants with a fundamental problem: receiving money for regular transactions. A credit card had card details that could be used to identify an account for a transaction, but how would one protect this information and prevent it from abuse?

At the time, several options were competing for being the primary means of exchange on the Internet. The big card providers were in the game, but PayPal also presented a coherent vision. In 1999 two other companies joined the emerging payment space of the Internet, Flooz and Beenz. These were altogether different visions than the ones we had seen before. Flooz's vision was to establish a currency for Internet merchants similar to frequent flier programs. Users could get Flooz credits either as awards by merchants or by purchasing them from the Flooz website. But the pattern repeated itself: by 2001, the FBI notified that it was used for money laundering; a Russian-Filipino crime syndicate was buying and spending credits with stolen credit cards. The company closed in the summer of 2001, leaving more than 300,000 customers with worthless Flooz credits.

Beenz was the leading competitor. It was conceptualized as a micro-currency that would reward people for their attention and for performing different actions online. Once the users had gained credits, they could be sold or spent. Beenz branded itself as the Web's currency and consequently saw itself investigated for running an unlicensed bank. The company insisted that it was merely virtual points. It folded after further funding failed to materialize when the dot-com bubble burst in 2001.

These are examples of currencies tailored more to the preferences and convenience of the general consumer and merchant than to secure privacy. Still, they suffered many of the same weaknesses, such as exposure to fraudulent use and regulatory challenges.

From Digital Postage to Money

Along with the spread of the Internet came email. Shifting from physical mail to electronic mail made communication easy. Too easy, in fact. The consequence of letting people send mail to anyone free of charge is spam. In the old physical world, it was not impossible to send mail to everyone, but there was a natural limit since each letter had a small cost defined by postage. The purpose of Hashcash was similarly to create a method to incur expenses on sending an email. Since postage is not dissimilar to bank notes, this in turn could be the basis more generally for producing a virtual currency. From this unlikely source, the solution for how to produce Bitcoin was born.

In May 1997, the British engineer Adam Back proposed a mechanism for "(...) throttling the systematic abuse of un-metered internet resources such as email." He called this Hashcash. This system generated a token as so-called proof of work, a concept we will return to. In short, it consists of solving a mathematical challenge difficult enough to warrant significant use of CPU power. This naturally has a cost in terms of energy and time. Thus, the Hashcash token is unlike previous examples of virtual currency pegged to or representing some other currency or precious metal. It expresses value only insofar as it was costly to produce.

Furthermore, Hashcash was not conceived as money but as postage. This could, however, be generalized into money. Back also speculated along these lines and suggested that tokens could be bought and sold through an anonymous ecash system like David Chaum's. Some could then specialize in what would later be known as mining Hashcash tokens that they would sell to others to use. The problem was that a token could be used only once and somebody had to track whether it was already used.

Hal Finney picked up on the idea of Adam Back. Finney wasn't just anybody and would later be central to the development and success of Bitcoin. He had been part of the cypherpunk and cryptography mailing lists. He was intimately involved in the extropian movement, which dreamt of a future on the other side of the singularity where cryogenics would mean you could be resurrected. But if you were to be resurrected in a couple of hundred years, a primary concern would be ensuring you had some cash to live from, and banks and governments naturally could not be trusted.

Consequently, a private digital cash system was a central quest of this future vision. Finney had been involved in more than a few ideas about such. He proposed a method by which these tokens could be used again as reusable proof-of-work (RPOW) tokens. This would transfer the Hashcash tokens from a form of expendable postage type of tokens to real reusable currency tokens that could function as a virtual currency.

Decentralizing the Bank

The problem with all earlier virtual currencies was that they always depended in one way or another on a central entity that you would have to trust. Cypherpunks were no more trusting of each other than banks and governments. This central entity could, in principle, meddle with the balances of accounts or otherwise interfere with the money supply. The challenge was, therefore, to devise a system to circumvent the need to have any central authority altogether.

Working on the problem of creating the currency for the future crypto anarchy envisioned by Tim May in his *The Crypto Anarchist Manifesto*, Wei Dai sketched a few key properties such a currency should have. According to Dai, the solution was that the entire ledger with balances of all accounts was distributed in a network. The currency was called B-money. A transaction was made between a seller and a buyer through cryptographic proof. This transaction would then be promoted throughout the network. Dai speculated about the value of B-money tokens and suggested that they would be pegged to the money it cost to generate them. This was possible since the mechanism was similar to the Hashcash proof-of-work mechanism. Although Satoshi would later cite this in the Bitcoin whitepaper, it was nothing more than a few paragraphs of speculation on his website. It had nothing of the detail and rigor of Hashcash and referenced ideas others had described before, in particular, Hashcash (which Adam Back also immediately pointed out to Dai on the cryptography mailing list). The idea of a decentralized open ledger, however, was novel.

Another critical actor in this space was Nick Szabo, a computer scientist who had worked in the virtual currency area for many years and was also a member of the cryptography mailing list. He had even been an early employee in David Chaum's DigiCash and had gained a reputation for eclectic and innovative thinking. He presented an idea he called Bitgold. This was similar to Dai's B-money, a speculative sketch on his blog that was never implemented. Bitgold would be a store of value like gold that could be produced by dedicating one's computer in a network to solve cryptographic puzzles in the same manner as Hashcash and B-money. Solved puzzles would be sent to a public registry and assigned to the user. These would be part of the next puzzle foreshadowing the blockchain of Bitcoin. A particular focus was on the problem of double spending, since the problem with digital tokens is whether they have already been used. This idea, like Dai's, was presented in a few short blog posts and never worked out in any detail, but pointed to central concepts and visions that would be picked up by Bitcoin.

The Three Strains of Virtual Currencies

In the space of a decade, several virtual currencies came and went. The different proposals were varied and innovative, some borrowing from each other or reflecting similar ideas. It is possible to distinguish three distinct strains of innovation in virtual currencies, all departing from different points. The first, the gold strain, was focused on the digital representation of precious metals; the second, the ecommerce strain, was on online shopping and awards in the shape of points and tokens; and the third, the crypto strain, is the one that turned into bitcoin and subsequent cryptocurrencies with a focus on privacy. These three strains needed more direct interaction regarding people and ideas. They also appealed to different segments of users. But they tried to solve similar problems, how to represent and exchange value virtually. They also ran into precisely the same regulatory and security issues, affecting each other through learning.

The first question to ask was, why precisely at this point did virtual currencies appear? As we saw, the idea of a virtual currency was a familiar one. It was envisioned early on, even in a sense, by Hayek in the 1920s. While personal computers did exist and began to be used widely in the

1980s, they were not generally connected to anything. Only in the mid- or late 1990s did connection to the Internet become common. Since the Internet was a precondition for a virtual currency, this created the possibility for new financial innovations.

Let us consider the gold strain of virtual currencies that focused on a currency somehow pegged to gold in particular or other precious metals. By now, it should come as no surprise that primarily the libertarian community was deeply engaged in bringing forth and using virtual currencies. For many libertarians, the abolition of the gold standard of money was a key grudge against central banks and governments. They felt that this move made it possible for governments to rob the people of the value of their money through inflation created by an increased money supply. Therefore, it should be no surprise that owning gold and other precious metals as a hedge against inflation was a key objective. While the Liberty dollar was more of an ideological statement than a practical way to transact in a gold-based currency, e-gold became a significant corporation with billions of dollars of value going through it in transactions. Around ten companies appeared with a similar focus of making it possible for ordinary people to own and trade precious metals by themselves. One of them, eBullion, was even integrated into a credit card for payment before it reverted into fraud and disappeared. Others turned out to be scams or succumbed to the increased regulatory attention given to them. A few, however, managed to adapt to the changing regulatory demands and thrive until this day but not as a virtual currency.

One significant effect of this strain on the crypto strain was the severe legal issues in which Liberty dollar and e-gold found themselves. This reverberated through the cryptography and cypherpunk mailing lists for years and may be the direct cause of Satoshi presenting his ideas under a pseudonym: no one wanted to spend years in legal jeopardy facing 20 years in prison for trying to bring forth a new innovative idea.

The ecommerce strain was more of an afterthought brought about by the change of the Internet from a place for information exchange to one for the exchange of goods. It served the regular participants of commerce, shoppers, and merchants with no particular political axe to grind who just wanted convenience. Online credit card payments had yet to mature; the door was open for other potential currencies to pay. The model was the loyalty program that had served retailers and airlines well. Points, tokens, and vouchers, after all, already functioned as a specialized currency within loyalty programs, so it took a lot of work to rethink these as a general currency to be used across companies. This movement however suffered from the same examples of criminal abuse and regulatory attention as well as the collapse of the dot-com bubble. They survived though in the shape of loyalty programs mostly of type 1 or type 2 virtual currencies (internal or unidirectional), and some even created de facto local virtual currencies that could be used across different companies. But with the emergence of credit cards and PayPal as viable and reasonably convenient methods of payment, the thrust for innovation for a general type 3 (bidirectional) virtual currency for ecommerce disappeared.

The community for whom a virtual currency was most central were the cypherpunks or extropians. These were technically savvy people with a firm belief in a radically different and better future for which the current currencies of governments would not work. For them, privacy was the central concern. We saw how works of fiction shaped the expectations of such an utterly private currency that could secure the user's anonymity. The goal was to create a payment method that would not allow any government, bank, or other third party to know what anyone had purchased. Possibly due to a general distrust of the government, this fused with similar regrets of the libertarians in terms of monetary policy, in particular, the inflationary nature of contemporary money supply and a dislike of fractional banking. This community was the one that had the technical knowledge to put together an altogether new type of type 3 virtual currency that was not related to anything other the proof of work that made it challenging to produce new coins through the process of what came to be known as mining. More motivated by futuristic ideas of a techno-utopia than practical applicability, it laid the foundation for Bitcoin. It was always a niche undertaking by a relatively small number of people with specialized knowledge of cryptography, mathematics, and engineering skills. Even if the discussions and ideas thrown around were not always quite civil, the people were the type to grind it out until a solution was found eventually. This crypto strain of virtual currencies is where Bitcoin arose. All the ideas that came together in Bitcoin were already proposed before and highlighted in this chapter. But before we attempt to understand the inner workings of Bitcoin, we need to consider some of the technical solutions that made it possible.

CHAPTER 2

Cryptography

Bitcoin gave rise to the specific type of virtual currency known as cryptocurrency. The reason for this name is the extended use of cryptography. A fundamental purpose of cryptography is to maintain confidentiality and integrity in communication, which is done through encryption. In cryptography, the message to be communicated is called the plain text and can be read by anyone who understands the language. The encrypted message is called the ciphertext and will not be intelligible to anyone.

There are many different ways to encrypt a message. The simplest and one of the earliest is called the Caesar cipher because Julius Caesar used it in the Gallic wars to send messages between army units. When you use this technique, all the letters in the plain text are shifted by a fixed number of places in the alphabet. The number of places the ciphertext is shifted in the alphabet is the key used for encryption. If +3 is used as an encryption key, a letter in the plain text is shifted three places to the right in the ciphertext.

The plain text "hello world" would produce the ciphertext "khoor zroug." Consequently, even if the encrypted message, the ciphertext, were intercepted, it would be unintelligible to the interceptor. Only if the interceptor knew the algorithm (shifting the letters) and the key (+3) would they be able to decrypt it.

This type of encryption might have fooled the Romans' enemies two thousand years ago, but today it would not fool anyone for long. While the discipline of encoding messages is called cryptography, the field of breaking codes is called cryptanalysis. The cryptanalyst uses different

A. Lisdorf, *Still Searching for Satoshi*, https://doi.org/10.1007/978-1-4842-9639-4_2

techniques to break the ciphertext and try to find the key. An example of this is looking at letter frequencies. If the language of the plain text is known, it is easy to find the most frequent letter in the ciphertext and assume that this represents the most frequent letter in the language of the plain text. There are several other structures to look for in a language, such as what letters often follow others and standard phrases.

If correspondences between probable plain text letters and ciphertext values can be found, looking at the shift between them in the alphabet gives away the key when a Caesar cipher is used, and it is possible to decrypt the entire ciphertext.

The Caesar cipher uses what is called a symmetric key. It is called such because it uses the same key to encrypt and decrypt the plain text. Cryptography and cryptanalysis have resulted in an ever-increasing arms race that has pushed the techniques used for encryption to be ever more complex. In World War II, this arms race between German cryptographers and British cryptanalysts took center stage. After World War I, the Germans introduced the Enigma cipher, which gave them the upper hand against the British cryptanalysts. The Enigma machine was complex and depended on a significant number of mechanical transformations, but the Germans assumed that at some point, the enemy would get hold of the device, so they designed it such that without the initial settings and the key, the messages could not be decrypted. At Bletchley Park, the British cryptanalysts tried frantically to deduce the key, but since the Enigma machine worked with a day key that was changed each day, it made all progress during the day worthless when the day was over. The next day a new day key was used, and the work started all over from scratch. Eventually, though, this key was also intercepted by the capture of a German codebook.

Symmetric encryption works well in a context where the communicating parties know each other and have agreed on a key in advance or if they can exchange the key through a secure channel. Such a channel is usually much more limited in terms of bandwidth and delay.

If, for example, the Gauls were to obtain or guess the key used by Caesar, the key would be compromised, and messages encrypted with it could no longer be considered confidential. Now Caesar would have to reconvene all army unit commanders and agree on a new key or send a dispatcher to them with the new key. This process is not convenient since it will take time. Similarly, for the Germans, the codebook must be distributed in a secure channel, but even that could be compromised.

The weakness of symmetric encryption is thus that it is necessary to share a key first in a secure channel before a secure communication can be initiated. This channel is likely to be constrained in terms of bandwidth and delay. It is also always at risk of being intercepted by an eavesdropper.

Public Key Encryption

During World War II, an arms race took place in cryptography. Still, even if it that led to ever more sophisticated encryption, it was symmetric encryption and, as we just saw, that requires a prior distribution of a shared key for encryption and decryption. This is known as the key distribution problem, which had been considered impossible to solve for thousands of years.

Diffie-Hellman-Merkle

Around the middle of the 1970s, one of the most fruitful partnerships in cryptography started. Whitfield Diffie had been thinking about the key distribution problem for a while. In 1974 he was invited to IBM's Thomas J. Watson Laboratory to give a talk about various strategies for attacking the key distribution problem. After the talk, he was told that a Stanford professor named Martin Hellman had recently visited and was working on the same problem. Diffie joined Hellman in California, and they immediately found common ground. They were looking for a way to arrive at a common key without ever exchanging it. They worked together with Ralph Merkle on this problem. After two years without any progress, Hellman came up with a solution. It works like this: Alice and Bob agree on a mathematical one-way function. Alice picks a private key (say 3) and generates a public key (4) using the function. Alice then sends this key to Bob. He generates his own private key (5) and uses the same function to generate a public key (6) that he sends to Alice.

Alice then takes Bob's public key and her own private key to generate the encryption key (9). Bob similarly takes Alice's public key and his own private key to generate the encryption key (9). Now the beauty of the mathematical function that Hellman found was that it ensured that Alice and Bob would thus be able to generate the same key (9) without it ever being shared publicly. Moreover, even if an eavesdropper, Eve, intercepted the entire communication, she would not be able to generate the key since Alice and Bob's private keys are necessary to do that. The resulting process is known as the Diffie-Hellman-Merkle key exchange and was the first time a solution to the key distribution problem was published.

This significantly improved the possibility of secure encryption since the confidentiality of the key was always the Achilles heel of cryptography. With the advent of modern telecommunications, things started to change in how we share information. It became more ubiquitous and easy. Still, even with Diffie -Hellman-Merkle key exchange, you would have to wait for the reply of the person you communicated with, and the encryption and decryption was done with the same key. It was, therefore, still traditional symmetric key encryption that required key distribution.

Consequently Whitfield Diffie continued thinking about the problem of key exchange. If he could find a solution where the encryption key differed from the decryption key, key distribution would be dispensed with altogether. Diffie eventually found a way this could be done. It was published in the seminal paper by Whitfield Diffie and Martin E. Hellman titled "New Directions in Cryptography" in 1976. They noted that with modern telecommunication (or teleprocessing as they called it), an increased burden arose on the key distribution channels. Finding secure channels and establishing a shared key before communication could start was cumbersome, especially between parties that did not know each other in advance. Technologies like the telephone, telex, and the Internet have high speed and bandwidth compared with other sources but are easy to wiretap. It is impossible to be confident that there is no eavesdropping.

The paper argued that two problems needed to be solved: privacy and authentication. Privacy was to be solved with public key encryption and authentication with a digital signature.

Diffie and Hellman suggested a method from which two keys could be constructed from a random number: a public and a private key. The public key can be shared over nonsecure channels and used to encrypt messages that can only be decrypted with the private key. Note the difference between Diffie-Hellman-Merkle key exchange and actual asymmetric encryption. In the former, a back-and-forth is necessary to ensure encryption. In the latter, this is not needed as long as the receiver's public key is known. This would eventually be a key feature for making it convenient to send money with Bitcoin: only the receiver's public key is necessary rather than a cumbersome back-and-forth exchange to generate a shared key.

The RSA Paper

Diffie and Hellman could, however, not prove in detail how to achieve that. That would only be done the following year, in 1977, when Ron Rivest, Adi Shamir, and Leonard Adleman published their groundbreaking paper "A Method for Obtaining Digital Signatures and Public-Key Cryptosystems." The computer scientist Ron Rivest worked at MIT on the other end of the country and read the Diffie-Hellman paper. He was fascinated and tried to get his colleagues, Adi Shamir, also a computer scientist, and Leonard Adleman, a mathematician, interested. Initially, they were not too enthusiastic. They tried different possibilities and almost lost hope that the function Diffie and Hellman looked for could be found. But in the spring of 1977, Rivest came upon an idea that would work.

The algorithm would be known as the RSA algorithm based on the authors' surnames. They suggested doing this based on prime factorization. It works by finding two very large prime numbers. These are the private key. Factoring them together generates a public key. Anyone could use this to encrypt a message. The function used to encrypt is a one-way function, which means it cannot be decrypted using the same key. The only key that can be used is the private key.

Public key encryption, in general, works by creating two mathematically related keys: a public key and a private key. You can now display the public key for anyone to use to encrypt messages for you. The resulting ciphertext can now only be decrypted with the private key belonging to the public key that was generated in the key pair. It follows that anyone could display their public key for people to use for encrypted communication without any previous engagement. This model suited the new world of ubiquitous and easily accessible telecommunication.

A British Twist

About 20 years later, it was discovered that the invention of such a system was made already in the early 1970s by British cryptographers working for the UK Government Communications Headquarters (GCHQ). By the end of the 1960s, British intelligence started working on the key distribution problem since key distribution was seen as a key part of the future of battlefield communication. They imagined a future where every soldier could use encrypted communication. This would make key distribution problematic.

James H. Ellis was given the task of looking into the key distribution problem. He eventually conceived of the idea like Diffie and Hellman did and proved that it was possible, but he could not find the mathematical function to do it. For years GCHQ worked on identifying this function. In 1973 a new young mathematician by the name of Clifford Cocks was given the task to try and find the function that would make asymmetric cryptology possible. He almost immediately found the function using primes and effectively found the RSA algorithm years before it was found by Ron Rivest.

Working for the military, they did not realize that this would have any general applicability, which is also why it was kept secret until 1997, when it was declassified by the British government. This system was viewed more as a curiosity than an important innovation since it depended on what, at the time, was extensive computing power. Development in computer technology made this feasible in the following decades. Thus, a convergence of increased computing power and mathematical breakthroughs made asymmetric encryption possible around the end of the 1970s.

Bringing Public Key Cryptography to the Masses

The military background and application would come back to haunt the development of public key cryptography. While the general approach was published in the RSA paper, the details were not accessible since they were top secret in the case of British intelligence and protected by a patent in the case of the RSA algorithm. There was no publicly available version.

As the Internet became available to a more significant amount of people and the computing power of personal computers grew steadily through the 1980s, public key encryption became possible in principle for a wider audience. The government had historically employed cryptography for military and diplomatic purposes. But with the advent of the Internet and email, a new problem arose. In the time of physical letters, it was possible for the government or other actors to eavesdrop on conversations by opening and closing letters. This could not be done at scale since there was a physical limit to how many letters could be opened and read. With email, this was not the case. The government could easily read every email sent in plain text and even search for keywords. This fact bothered certain people who were not trusting of the government's intentions.

It motivated the American computer scientist Phil Zimmerman to develop a program based on the principles of the Diffie-Hellman article that would make it possible to use public-private key encryption in an accessible way. He believed regular people had a right to privacy and called the program Pretty Good Privacy or PGP encryption.

Zimmerman shared it on the Internet, where it quickly gained traction. It seemed to be a success until two years later when the US Customs Service initiated a criminal investigation of Zimmerman. At the time, encryption was still understood as a military matter and consequently subject to arms trafficking export controls. Since PGP was distributed over the Internet, it could be considered "munitions export without a license." This could have been the end of public availability of public key encryption schemes, but Zimmerman found an imaginative way around this by publishing the entire source code of his PGP program in a book. By doing this, he could refer to his first amendment right of freedom of speech.

While Bitcoin does not use PGP, it was favored by cypherpunks, and it was common for members of the cryptography mailing list to publish their PGP public key to be used for encrypted communication in email. It also demonstrated a blueprint for how public key encryption specifically and cryptographic systems in general could be leveraged for the Internet.

Public key encryption is a way to ensure confidentiality, that is, to protect the privacy of the plain text of a message. As such, it is not of central relevance to either the transmission or generation of bitcoins since all transactions are public. But it is used as a basis for other key features, such as digital signatures. Before we get to the details of that, we have to consider another crucial cryptographic function.

Hashing

A central function for the workings of Bitcoin is what is known as a hash function. A hash function is a function that takes an arbitrary-size data as input and generates a fixed, usually shorter, length output. This shorter output is called a hash.

Let us look at an example: using the hash algorithm MD5 (message digest), this text

An old silent pond…

A frog jumps into the pond,

splash! Silence again.

Autumn moonlight—

a worm digs silently

into the chestnut.

Lightning flash—

what I thought were faces

are plumes of pampas grass.

—Basho Matsuo

yields this hash: 5e477f116910df7e60d4ca527335a6e2.

That's one small step for man, one giant leap for mankind.

—Neil Armstrong

yields this hash: ee77e1ab9d67a32bcc00cf42d71b7ae7.

As can be seen, the resulting hash string is of precisely the same length. If we input Tolstoy's *War and Peace*, the hashing would still only result in the same size of the hash.

The hash function has the additional property that every time it is applied to the same input, it generates the same output. No matter where or when someone calculates the preceding inputs, they will result in the same hash. Furthermore, this calculation is not computationally intensive.

Moreover, even the slightest change in input to a hash function will result in a radically different output, as can be seen from the following example:

> "Where is my mind" yields this hash:
> a05f82ba995f3cb65d0947373387925b.

> "Where is my mint" yields this hash:
> d9f4f0831e1045363f14699ca8a9d4e6.

Not one character is the same in any position of the resulting output hash, whereas only one character (the last) differed in the input. It is also improbable that any other input will yield the same output, a phenomenon known as a hash collision.

The last important thing to observe is that a hash function is a one-way function, which cryptographers call a trapdoor. You can only go from input to output, not the other way. It is impossible to recreate the input from the output.

The mathematical function used in popular hashing algorithms like MD5, SHA-1, and SHA-2 is called a Merkle-Damgård construction. It was discovered by Ralph Merkle, the same Merkle who worked with Diffie and Hellman, in 1979 and later proven independently by Ivan Bjerre Damgård ten years later. This construction assures that any input can be compressed to a fixed length.

Ronald Rivest (one of the authors of the RSA paper) developed the MD2 (message digest) hashing function in 1989 and gradually improved it until MD5 in 1992, which was based on a 128-bit result. These were reasonably successful, but given that computing became increasingly powerful and cheap, the bar for what was considered secure continued to move.

Remember that a hash collision means that two different inputs create the same result. This is very unlikely but possible. A brute-force attack that tries a lot of possible combinations might need to try a high number of times. If this is done, it undermines the premise that a hash function proves that the hash is the output derived from an input.

With a hash function producing a hash of 128 bits (like the MD5), a brute-force attack needs only to try several random inputs to produce 128 identical bits. This was difficult at the time, but around 1993, the National Institute of Standards and Technology (NIST) was not confident in the security and developed the SHA (Secure Hash Algorithm) with a 160-bit result. This was later followed by SHA-1 and SHA-2, which are the most common and well-known, since they form the bedrock of encryption on the Internet and are used for secure communication technologies like web certificates, SSL, TLS, etc.

The MD5 and SHA-1 have now been shown to be susceptible to collision attacks and are no longer considered sufficient. The NIST is working on a SHA-3 with a different structure. This development is expected to continue with the increasing availability of computing power.

To sum up, hashing is a function to create a digest or fingerprint of a data input. This "fingerprint," like human fingerprints, is not necessarily unique and may be achieved by another input. This is called a collision. A collision can be achieved only by brute force, that is, trying a large number of different random inputs, and not incremental changes that will continuously get closer to the hash value. This is a crucial property of hashing that finds innovative use in Hashcash, as we shall see later in the "Proof of Work" section, but first we must return to digital signatures.

Digital Signature

Building on Diffie and Hellman's work, Rivest, Shamir, and Adleman also showed how their method could be used for signing a message. If Bob writes a message to Alice using Alice's public key for encryption, he can then use his private key to generate a signature of the text. Alice can then decode the message and verify that it was indeed Bob who signed it by using Bob's public key. This process is called non-repudiation, that is, proof that someone had to have signed this. Non-repudiation is particularly important in the case of contracts and transfers of money. The digital signature proves that this particular text was signed with this particular private key belonging to the public key of a known owner.

One of the missing pieces of the puzzle to achieve a digital signature scheme was a convenient way to sign a message. Signing it in its entirety was computationally intensive, so another approach was needed. The message could be reduced before it was signed. Instead of signing the entire message, one can create a hash of the message. As we saw previously, this is a fingerprint that, with very high probability, cannot be produced by another input. The fingerprint thus represents the message. This hash can then be encrypted with the author's private key.

Using the author's public key to decrypt the signature yields the hash. The original plain text message can then be hashed, and the resulting hash can be compared to the one derived from the signature. If it is identical, it proves that the owner of the private key belonging to the author's public key encrypted the message, or more simply, the author wrote precisely this message.

This effect can be used for different things. First of all, it can be used for documenting the wording of a contract, for example. If two parties to a contract do not have identical versions, it can be proven with mathematical certainty which version is correct: the one yielding the hash that was signed. Second, it can be used to document the integrity of the message, that is, no one inserted anything into the message during transit or afterward.

Digital signatures are, therefore, more efficient than regular ones since they prove that the signer signed the document and the particular shape of the document. This is a feature that we will see in many applications of the blockchain.

Proof of Work

Unfortunately, privacy was not the only new problem email introduced into digital communication. Another problem with the networked world was derived precisely from its purpose: to make communication immediate, easy, and free at any distance to any number of people. Bypassing traditional barriers for communication, such as printing and distributing books and newspapers and writing and posting emails, proved liberating for most, but the downside was that it opened for new phenomena that these barriers had kept in check: scams.

When I was a child, I remember that sometimes you would receive a note that you won some German lottery and you just had to pay for the lottery ticket or something. Of course, this was not true but a scam to get money from people. It was, however, relatively rare because mailing a letter was not free. The economics of the scam had to make sure that a significant percentage of people would pay. If the postage of a letter was $0.50 and the scam would yield $100, only 200 letters could be sent out. This means that the conversion had to be 1 in 200.

With the advent of email, these economics changed. If a letter costs $0.0001 (allowing for some funds to cover the Internet connection and domain registration), the conversion rate now only has to be 1 in 1,000,000. Not only scams could now be economically distributed; any kind of advertising or political propaganda could be communicated at this price point compared to comparable rates for advertising in newspapers or TV. This gave rise to the phenomenon of spam, which still haunts us today.

The root cause of this is not that people suddenly became more susceptible or open to advertisement and fraud. Instead it is the simple fact that the cost of communicating had been lowered so much that even meager success rates became profitable. Since it would be against the very idea of the Internet to begin to tax communication, it was necessary to start thinking about it differently. If it was possible to incur a price on the sender but not the receiver as in the old model of communication, it would be possible to change the dynamic and limit spam by making it more costly.

Combating Junk Mail

Again the world of cryptography came to the rescue. In 1993 Cynthia Dwork and Moni Naor presented an idea to impose what they called a pricing function to combat junk mail. They recognized that the cost of electronic communication would not be a deterrent and that implementing any legal restrictions would not be feasible. Instead, they looked for another type of cost on transmission: "The main idea is for the mail system to require the sender to compute some moderately expensive, but not intractable, function of the message and some additional information." The cost would here be imposed by the price of computation, that is, from hardware and electricity. This idea is what would later be known as proof of work.

The problem seems similar to the one-way functions of encryption. We saw how they were easy to decrypt with the key but almost impossible without. We still want the same asymmetry where it is easy for one party (the receiver) and hard for the other party (the sender), but we don't want to make it too hard. The quest was, therefore, for a way to adjust the difficulty of the problem through a parameter.

To make the function predictable and not depend on the length of the email, they suggested the function should be based on the hash function, which, as we saw, always yields a string of the same size.

Based on this input, the pricing function should be able to turn the difficulty of computing the result up and down through some parameter. The result should be easy to check. They suggested three families of functions but remarked that further research was needed since cryptography, until then, had paid little attention to moderately hard functions. All attention had been on developing virtually unbreakable functions.

Applying Proof of Work

It was not until 1999 that this idea was formalized and given the name proof of work in an article by Markus Jakobsson and Ari Juels. They note several different ways that proof of work can be used. One of them is as a way to control the delay. This type of usage aims to control how long it will take to solve the cryptographic problem. Such use had been developed in 1996 by Rivest, Shamir (of the RSA paper), and Wagner, which they called a time-lock puzzle.

Rivest and Shamir also developed an application of proof of work, which they called MicroMint. This was, in fact, a cryptosystem designed for micropayments over the Internet. They describe the scheme thus: "MicroMint "coins" are produced by a broker, who sells them to users. Users give these coins to vendors as payments. Vendors return coins to the broker in return for payment by other means. A coin is a bit-string whose validity can be easily checked by anyone but which is hard to produce."

As a method of doing this, they suggested hash function collisions. Recall that a hash collision is a situation where two different inputs to a hash function yield the same output, that is, the same hash. In the article, they showed that it is possible to control how difficult such a collision should be.

In this scheme, a broker produces MicroMint "coins," which are bought by a customer, who purchases something from a vendor who redeems the value from the broker. The problem in this setup is the one that would be discussed frequently in the cryptographic community in relation to digital currencies, namely, that of double spending, because how would the vendor know that the "coin" was not already spent and redeemed by another vendor?

Digital Postage

Adam Back picked up on this challenge. He started to work on the Hashcash system already in 1997. The Hashcash solution has a function that computes a token. His solution allowed us to dynamically adjust the difficulty of producing Hashcash tokens. These tokens are similar to the MicroMint coins suggested by Rivest and Shamir. Unfortunately, like them, he had no solution for the double spending problem other than keeping track of it in a centralized database. Through Hashcash, Back sought to provide a mechanism whereby it would be possible to throttle un-metered Internet resources such as email. Even though he hinted that it could be used for digital cash, it was not explicitly generalized toward that end. That and the solution to the double spending problem would not come until ten years later with the proposal of Bitcoin.

Adding Cost to Free Information

Proof of work was a consequence of the falling costs of mass communication. It introduced a way to use cryptographic functions to provide puzzles that would require a predictable expenditure of CPU. This, in turn, translated into cost. A variable cost could now be added to previously free functions. The problem with doing this with email was that no system ever gained widespread adoption. Instead, the industry focused on spam detection and blacklisting mechanisms to eliminate spam. If it were not for the application of proof of work later in Bitcoin and subsequent blockchains, it might have been confined to the already extensive rarity section of cryptography.

How Crypto Became Currency

Cryptography had been a niche discipline with little change over two millennia. It was confined mainly to the interest of military and government diplomacy. If someone had suggested, for example, in the beginning of the 1960s that cryptography would become central for a worldwide digital communication network and a new kind of currency, the response might well have been a slight giggle and rolling of the eyes.

But all that changed in the 1970s. The advent of the modern computer and more focused application of mathematical theory led to a momentous shift that changed cryptography and digital communication. The discovery of public key cryptography and hashing paved the way for innovations that today underpin much of the information infrastructure of the Internet. It also formed the bedrock against which the dreams of a digital currency could be realized so much so that this type of currency would come to be known as cryptocurrency.

It was, however, not sufficient. As we saw, such cryptocurrencies had been proposed around the turn of the millennium, but some problems remained, most notably the double spending problem, that is, how to prove that a token or coin had not already been spent. Another problem was centralization since all proposed models depended in one way or another on a centralized third party that had to be trusted. This was a significant weakness that the cypherpunks were well aware of and not ready to gloss over since this was similar to the dreaded banks' role as central gatekeepers of your money. To deliver the full promise of a genuinely free virtual currency, a few more pieces of the puzzle had to be solved. We will now turn our attention to them.

CHAPTER 3

Public Record

For millennia, humans had to establish a shared indisputable truth. In oral societies, this was typically done through rote learning and performance. A typical example of how oral societies established such shared public truth can be found in classical antiquity. The poets of ancient Greece, like Hesiod and Homer, are representative of a rich oral tradition. The verse was not an artistic outlet for creative innovation. Quite the contrary. Ancient Greece glorified the past, not the future. It was the primary technology to establish a shared public record of the past.

Reciting verses established near-identical versions of heroic deeds and ancient myths across time and space. The verse meter was a mnemonic technique employed for the bard to be able to recite the information in the same manner everywhere he went and teach others so they could replicate the same record of heroic deeds and myth. They could remember and recite tens of thousands of lines, but it was still not a very efficient way to establish a shared public record, as the many diverging versions of Greek myth show. Only when writing was employed could a public record be committed to posterity without the intervention of any particular person's memory.

© Anders Lisdorf 2023
A. Lisdorf, *Still Searching for Satoshi*, https://doi.org/10.1007/978-1-4842-9639-4_3

The Earliest Writing and Single-Entry Bookkeeping

The process of creating a written shared public record started millennia before the works of Hesiod and Homer were written down. The first examples of writing are from the fourth millennium BCE in the form of the cuneiform clay tablets from ancient Mesopotamia, present-day Iraq. This area is known as the fertile crescent and was the cradle of the earliest known human civilizations.

The cuneiform writing was pictographic, consisting of pictures and marks of different forms. The tablets did not contain accounts of myths or heroic deeds but rather something as pedestrian as records of livestock, grain, and corn. It was a public record of ownership and was used for three millennia in different languages across the ancient Middle East. There was a gradual change to incorporate syllables and other symbols, but the primary use case was the same: documenting ownership in a public record. This function is thus even more primitive than writing and predates prose texts about myths and laws by millennia. Consequently, we must deal with a powerful and essential technology for human civilization.

Whereas the purpose of cryptography is to obfuscate and hide information, the purpose of a public record is the opposite: to document and elevate information to the level of shared indisputable truth. Putting it on clay or other stone mediums rather than softer and more mutable media like papyrus, animal skin, or wax tablets made information immutable. This is particularly handy when establishing truth in the face of competing versions, which you would need when it involves ownership of something of value. A technique that makes the record immutable is a prerequisite for it to serve as the basis of ownership documentation.

If the records could be changed at will, the information would not be suitable to establish the truth. Thus, stone served for millennia as the medium of choice and engraving of signs as the technology for establishing a public record. We still see remnants of this today on memorials, gravestones, and religious shrines. These are all examples of information that someone wishes to commit to posterity and raise beyond dispute. However, it is no longer the technology of choice for documenting economic transactions.

With the expansion of the population in cities and the resulting expansion in economic output, the volume of transactions increased to a size that no longer made it practical to document everything on bulky and heavy clay tablets. The information that could be recorded on one slab was low compared with its size and weight. Other technologies like papyrus and animal skin gained popularity as they were lighter and took up less space. The ratio of information content to weight and physical volume was higher. The need to document the information for hundreds or thousands of years that the stone medium supported was, in most cases, not needed when it came to financial transactions. As a result, these lighter mediums gradually became important for documenting financial information. From antiquity to medieval times, they remained the chosen format for creating financial records. This was the technology of the discipline that would come to be known as accounting.

The Mesopotamian system was called a single-entry bookkeeping system or cash-based accounting. It documented transactions as entries on a list.

The Accounting Revolution and Double-Entry Bookkeeping

Single-entry bookkeeping is undoubtedly superior to having no system for documentation. Still, it is also liable to errors and fraud since there is no check on the entry into the system. It is impossible to investigate whether any single entry is correct or who made the entry. Therefore, single-entry accounting systems are only viable for enterprises where perfect trust is in place, like a household. When there is always just a single transaction entry, the enterprise must trust that it is done correctly. This was indeed the case for most of history, but it was necessary to improve this system of accounting to achieve further economic development.

The Romans developed many essential techniques for managing accounting, but medieval times saw a reduction in complex economic activity, and those techniques seem to have been forgotten. Only in the developments of Renaissance Italy would a revolution in accounting take shape. With their mercantile prowess and global ambition, the city-states of Florence, Genoa, and Venice became the centers of developing the next step in establishing a record of financial activity. It was here that the practice of double-entry bookkeeping was developed. These principles are still adhered to today in modern enterprises.

The earliest examples of double-entry bookkeeping can be traced to the thirteenth century, although even the Romans practiced it in some form. The Roman writer Pliny the Elder described the practice around 70 CE. Still, it wasn't until the end of the fifteenth century, when Luca Pacioli described it in his *Summa de arithmetica, geometria, proportioni et proportionalita* in 1494, that it became a well-described standard that subsequent generations of accountants would use.

Double-entry bookkeeping aims to account for all transactions of money to detect errors and fraud. One transaction in double-entry bookkeeping always affects two accounts. These have two sides: debit and credit.

The transaction will appear as debit on one account and credit on another. If a merchant buys products from a supplier, the payment will show up as credit on the supplier's account and debit on the merchant's account for purchased goods. When sold, it will be debited to a customer account and credited to the purchased goods account.

If, on the other hand, a posting is made to the purchased goods account to credit it, indicating that something has been sold, but no debit record is made on any other account, it could mean that somebody pocketed the money somewhere.

Debit and credit accounts are supposed to balance if all transactions have been recorded correctly. If not, it is a sign that there is an error. The double-entry system thus provides the possibility of auditing past transactions.

This system became the standard among merchants of the Italian city-states around the time when their mercantile empires transformed Europe from a stagnant medieval patchwork of local competing powers to the center of a global trade network. The clarity and insight into a company's financial transactions helped lift trade from a local occurrence to a sizeable global affair. It was not the only factor, but it was critical in laying a foundation for the modern world through companies such as the Dutch East India Company, which built a global trade network and became the first common stock company. Transparent accounting practices makes it easier to understand why investors would have invested so much in this. Accounting practices helped bring clarity into the economic transactions performed by a company. With double-entry bookkeeping, it was possible to audit the books and spot fraud and errors, and someone external could audit the company.

Information Technology and Triple-Entry Bookkeeping

Less a new revolution, like the movement from single-entry bookkeeping to double-entry bookkeeping, the idea of triple-entry bookkeeping was meant as an extension. The sense that something was missing in the double-entry system started appearing by the end of the twentieth century.

For decades, Carnegie Mellon professor Yuji Ijiri had worked on different ideas about extending the double-entry bookkeeping system into other dimensions. He coined the term *triple-entry bookkeeping* to describe this. His idea was inspired by calculus and was also termed *momentum accounting*. It suggested that accounting should also keep track of the rate of change over time. He published these ideas in an essay in 1982.

The term, but not the idea, was picked up by Ian Grigg in 2005 in a paper titled "Triple Entry Accounting." The paper did not refer to Ijiri but similarly looked for ways to expand the double-entry bookkeeping system rather than replace it. Taking inspiration from the theory of database design developed by the English computer scientist Edgar F. Codd in the 1970s, he suggested another way of looking at accounting.

In relational database design, several criteria can be required for data organization. They are called normal forms. With every normal form, increasing constraints are placed on the design. The fourth normal form states that the other three must be fulfilled and that data should not contain multi-value dependencies. This means that all additional information can be derived from this data. In Grigg's words, "The principles of Relational Databases provide guidance here. The fourth normal form directs that we store the primary records, in this case, the set of receipts, and we construct derivative records, the accounting books, on the fly."

Let us try to open this statement up. Grigg was working in the space of cryptography, specifically on how to apply cryptography to accounting. Remember from the previous chapter that public key cryptography allowed digital data signage. We saw how it could be used for certifying a contract or other text. It could, however, also be used to authenticate a transaction. This is what Grigg means by a receipt: it is the transaction.

"In order to calculate balances on a related set of receipts, or to present a transaction history, a book would be constructed on the fly from the set. This amounts to using the Signed Receipt as a basis for single entry bookkeeping. In effect, the bookkeeping is derived from the raw receipts, and this raises the question as to whether to keep the books in place."

In this view, accounting could be done dynamically by calculating any set of receipts or transactions when needed. This system was meant to work through a central issuer who would, at any point in time, be able to calculate the balance of each customer the issuer handles dynamically based on all previous receipts. For example, a customer account could be dynamically calculated at any point in time, and the balance be known.

The transaction is, of course, something that already existed in traditional double-entry bookkeeping, but this was a private record used as input for posting. What is new here is that a public record of all previous transactions can be maintained cryptographically and signed by both parties. Once a receipt is finalized by signing from the two parties, it is part of a public record of transactions maintained by a central issuer who would always be able to calculate any account dynamically.

Grigg references earlier attempts at digital cash, such as DigiCash. Still, writing two years before the publication of the Bitcoin whitepaper, it is interesting to see that the idea of a public ledger of transactions was already being envisioned. Only Grigg's proposal was still managed by a central entity, an issuer, which is vulnerable to failure and corruption. Let us, therefore, turn to the next step in the journey toward Bitcoin decentralization.

Decentralizing the Record

The mode of recording and sharing the public record Grigg imagined for the issuer was on a server. The server is the central element in the client-server pattern in computing. A central instance, the server, performs the computational and data functions of the system for the clients. All clients can access the same central resources that the server makes available. This was how the first computers worked and also, to some extent, is how the Internet works today.

The web browser is the client that accesses the resources, the website, made available by the web server. This is a simple and efficient pattern, which accounts for its ubiquity. But it is also prone to central failure. If the central server is down, as in the case of a distributed denial-of-service attack, the whole system is down. This is a critical vulnerability for a system whose ambition is to be the source of a public record of economic transactions.

There is, however, another model. A peer-to-peer (or P2P for short) network is a network where nodes, or peers, connect directly to one another and form a mesh-type network rather than the hub-and-spoke type of the client-server model. There is no central instance that the system depends on. The idea of a peer-to-peer network goes back to the beginning of the Internet, but the present-day Internet is not such a network. The World Wide Web relies on a hierarchical system of name servers that resolve names into specific IP addresses. The IP addresses are the IDs of devices. In a peer-to-peer network, the computers need to know the IP addresses of the other nodes in the network since they do not rely on a central entity to resolve a name into an IP address.

The resulting network topology is a mesh network. This is a resilient type of network since it doesn't rely on any single point of failure. If one node fails, other nodes take over. If the average number of connections is high, the network is stable and resilient toward breakdowns.

The first to popularize P2P computing was Napster in 1999. In the 1990s, CDs still dominated music distribution, but a digital format had emerged called MP3 that made it possible to share songs digitally. Such songs could be copied to friends and family, but finding a friend who just happened to have any given song was difficult. Napster made it easy to share MP3 songs between strangers through peer-to-peer connections. They created a website where you could discover computers that were online with a particular song. The user would then connect to that computer and download it. This is the essence of a peer-to-peer network. It allows the illegal sharing of copyrighted material, which is why Napster was shut down already in 2001 due to legal issues. However, the principle of sharing directly with others through a decentralized network had been demonstrated and is still used today in services like BitTorrent.

The power of a P2P network in relation to file sharing is that as long as someone on the network has a copy of a file, the whole network has access to it. It does not rely on any central custodian or gatekeeper.

Leveraging P2P technology for bookkeeping carries some additional difficulties. The idea of documenting transactions as a public record carries with it the requirement of establishing the time of these transactions. Unlike digital songs, documenting when each transaction took place becomes of central importance. Since the timestamp of each transaction can be changed, it requires a solution.

Stuart Haber and Wakefield Stornetta were the first to solve this problem cryptographically in their 1990 paper "How to time-stamp a digital document" in the *Journal of Cryptology*. In this paper, they argued that the problem could be solved by establishing a Time-Stamping Service. To maintain privacy, it is not convenient for the user to send the entire document or other digital artifacts. Instead, the user uses a hash function to create a short fingerprint of the document, which is then signed by the Time-Stamping Service by appending a timestamp to the hash received. The certificate is then returned to the user. Anyone can now verify the timestamp based on this certificate without knowing the content of the document. Because the document is hashed with a date appended, it is impossible to retroactively alter the date since that would produce a different hash.

The problem here is that we still need to depend on a central authority. The Belgian cryptographer Jean-Jacques Quisquater came upon a solution to that problem around the same time. He suggested that the entire file, or chain of certificates, could be shared among a network of timestamp servers. The generated certificates did not contain confidential information and were, therefore, not sensitive. Any decentralized entity could add a timestamped document to this chain of timestamp certificates. This solution would solve the problem of timestamping transactions in a distributed public record.

A Decentralized Peer-to-Peer Public Record

Now we have come full circle. In Grigg's version of triple-entry accounting, a public record of transactions is maintained by a central issuer, which depends on a central server. Still, the public availability of it depends on whether the server is online. To make sure that the record is truly public and resilient to failure, it needs to be distributed. Hence, multiple entities have copies to prevent data loss, and multiple available nodes are online to secure availability in the event that one or more nodes fail. If one wanted to create a genuinely resilient public record, the optimal technology would be a P2P network.

A system that maintained economic transactions in an open-access ledger available to all nodes on a decentralized mesh network would make it virtually impossible to destroy the record of these transactions. If the immutability of the record were maintained by hashing, it would be similar to being cut in stone like the cuneiform tablets of Mesopotamia. The decentralized distribution would guarantee durability, which the stone also secured. As long as nodes are connected in a network, the record would be public and available for inspection.

Such a system could offer anyone access to the balances of every account that had ever been used for a transaction by dynamically querying the open ledger. It would no longer be necessary to carve the record in stone, and furthermore, it would be available through the Internet globally and not just locally, where the slabs of stone were stored. But the problem it solves is the same: to create an immutable and durable public record, not of heroic deeds in times past, but of economic activity to support exchange in the future.

CHAPTER 4

Bitcoin

Now we can start to piece together how Bitcoin works. The previous chapters allow us to understand better the diverse technologies and experiments with virtual currencies that made it possible for Bitcoin to appear at this particular time. Let us start with a simple outline of some key components of Bitcoin before we dive into the technical details that made them possible.

To put it simply, Bitcoin is a system that provides a virtual currency called bitcoin that users can exchange without any central intermediary like a bank, a company, or another organization. Bitcoin is divisible into eight decimal places (compare this with common currencies that are only divisible into two decimal places). The smallest unit is called a satoshi, similar to what the cent is to the dollar.

To start using bitcoin, a user needs to have a digital wallet. This wallet contains the public IDs the user can use to exchange bitcoin with other users. Its function is similar to what we know as an account that holds the bitcoin in the sense that you have a total of bitcoins to spend. It is only possible to get bitcoin into the wallet in two ways: either by creating bitcoin through the process of mining, which we will return to, or, the more common option, to have someone transfer bitcoin to your wallet. This last option can be done as payment for goods or services or through purchase.

It is still a minority who use bitcoin as means of payment though. When you purchase bitcoin, you transfer currency, such as dollars, to an intermediary who has bitcoin in their wallet to transfer to your wallet. This can be done through one of the bitcoin exchanges or anyone with a

© Anders Lisdorf 2023
A. Lisdorf, *Still Searching for Satoshi*, https://doi.org/10.1007/978-1-4842-9639-4_4

balance in their wallet. Another option is that bitcoin is purchased through another cryptocurrency, which is also common since bitcoin functions as a currency cross between the multitude of different cryptocurrencies that exist. These exchanges are external to the Bitcoin system. There are no dollars or any other currencies in the Bitcoin system.

So far, our intuitions from regular money and banking have held up: we have a currency traded in units that sum to a balance in a wallet, and transfers between wallets are possible. But here we start down the path where it gets positively strange compared with the traditional monetary system. All transactions that were ever made are recorded on a public ledger. This is what is known as the blockchain. The balance of any wallet is dynamically calculated by looking through all the ingoing and outgoing transactions (debit and credit) involving the wallet. There is, thus, no recorded balance anywhere; it is a calculated total based on the difference between inflow and outflow. The Bitcoin network will let the user spend the total at any given time. This is called a blockchain because, around every ten minutes, pending transactions on the network are packaged into a block that gets a number and a hash. This hash is used in the next block, thus forming a chain. This method ensures the integrity of the transactions in the chain of blocks going back to the very first block, called the Genesis block. We will return to the details later.

Now, this system needs someone to run it. A bank has central servers where all transactions are recorded and cleared, but Bitcoin instead has a network of nodes. This is a network of computers that all work on the same public record of transactions. The network picks up all transactions users want to make and records them in a block. These computers that run the Bitcoin network are called miners. They are rewarded with bitcoin for their work validating transactions. Any computer can, in principle, start mining bitcoin by downloading the open source Bitcoin software. Still, in practice, it is unlikely that a regular computer will ever produce any bitcoin since the mining task has become very specialized and requires custom-built chips to be able ever to get the reward. Remember that there is no reward for all the other computers that did not generate the block.

The miners compete to create the next block of transactions by trying to solve a cryptographic puzzle. This is a kind of proof of work and requires the expenditure of significant computing resources. The node on the network that first solves the puzzle and creates a block of transactions is rewarded with newly minted bitcoin. Each block generates a fixed amount of bitcoins as a reward.

This is a thumbnail sketch of Bitcoin and how it works to provide a general sense. Now let us dive into the details.

A Virtual Currency

Bitcoin picks up from the previous attempts at virtual currencies that went before it. It builds directly on the virtual currencies in the crypto strain of virtual currencies, where the emphasis is on privacy and a steady money supply. The Bitcoin whitepaper cites only two previous cryptocurrencies: Adam Back's Hashcash and Wei Dai's B-money. From Hashcash, it inherited the idea to employ proof of work to mint the currency. Much of Bitcoin's substance was already defined in Hashcash, so much so that Back would later say that he invented the bitcoin mining function, arguably a central component. Through bitcoin mining, the currency is produced and put into circulation like the Hashcash token, which is then subsequently ready for use in exchange.

One of the central concerns for many virtual currency proponents was the subversive role of banks, particularly central banks, because they "printed money" in the eyes of virtual currency believers. The increase in money supply created an inflationary effect, which in essence "steals" money from owners of currency because inflation reduces the value of nominal amounts of currency. In Bitcoin, the opposite had been planned.

A structural tightening of the money supply through the diminishing issuance of currency is designed to create a deflationary dynamic whereby the currency increases in value.

The supply of Bitcoin has a schedule through which less, not more, currency is produced over time. First, the theoretical amount of bitcoins that can be made is fixed in the design. In contrast to fiat currencies, which are the national currencies that people use in their daily lives such as dollars and euros, where the money supply is limitless, bitcoin is limited: there will only ever be 21 million bitcoins mined. After 50% of all bitcoins were mined, the first halving of the reward to miners occurred. That happened in 2012. After this, the reward was 25 bitcoins. The next halving occurred after 75% of all bitcoins were mined, after which the reward was 12.5 bitcoins. This will continue until there is no more bitcoin to put into circulation. According to calculations, the last bitcoin would be mined around 2140.

Building scarcity into the currency is probably inspired by the virtual currencies that built on precious metals since precious metals derive their value from scarcity. Gold is the most scarce of the three most common precious metals used for money historically: gold, silver, and bronze. Silver is the second most scarce and bronze the least. Conversely, a metal like iron is so ubiquitous that it does not hold much use as a store of value. Of particular interest in this regard is gold since the annual supply of gold to the world market has hovered around 2% of the total stock of gold for more than a hundred years. This situation creates a high stock-to-flow ratio, currently around 60, that is, the ratio of the total amount of gold in existence to newly mined gold. This dynamic is the reason that gold is better at holding its value. For silver, the stock-to-flow ratio is about 20, making it more abundant. This creates a different dynamic similar to the inflationary money supply. When too much is added to the total stock, each unit diminishes in value.

While e-gold, eBullion, and others traded electronic tokens pegged against real gold in storage, Nick Szabo suggested a purely digital version to create a digital store of value. Bitcoin eventually came close to the ideas Szabo presented in his thoughts on Bitgold. He imagined Bitgold being minted by solving a cryptographic puzzle, which creates a scarcity similar to that of gold. Solving the cryptographic puzzle would be similar to gold mining. Bitcoin was the first implementation of such a system.

Encrypting for Privacy

A key concern for cypherpunks was that of privacy. They took particular aim at the fact that banks and the government had disproportionate access to transactions made by customers. From these, a great deal of information can be gathered that is of private concern. Bitcoin, on the contrary, provides pseudonymous accounts by default, and no banks mediate transactions. Users cannot be identified directly by anyone based on their transactions.

The wallet is a central concept when we talk about Bitcoin, but it is more of a mental concept than a real technological artifact. Today a wallet is often synonymous with wallet software, which can take multiple forms. The wallet is either hosted by an online exchange or downloaded and run locally as a client application by the user. In one way, the term *wallet* is misleading because the wallet does not store any bitcoin. Engaging with the Bitcoin network to perform transactions requires some intermediary services. The wallet software provides these services, such as the ability to generate bitcoin addresses, store the private keys, and display the amount of bitcoins on each of your bitcoin addresses. This is necessary because Bitcoin is nothing more than a gigantic list of transactions.

To do anything with bitcoin, you first need an address, which is a string that identifies you to others and allows you to send and receive bitcoin. It can be thought of as a bank account; only with Bitcoin, you do not have to ask anyone to create one.

The address is based on cryptographic techniques we saw in Chapter 2. It is done the following way: First, a large random number is selected. This is your private key. Special care should be taken to protect this since this is all it takes to get access to your bitcoin. Based on this private key, a public key is generated through a technique called elliptic curve multiplication. This is the standard public-private key pair that can be used for encryption and signing. But we are not encrypting or signing anything just yet. Now, take the public key and run it through a one-way cryptographic hash function. First, the SHA-256 hash is computed from the public key, and from this value, a RIPEMD160 hash is calculated, which yields a 160-bit number. This is encoded as Base58Check, which renders the address a 58-character string. The result will be the address. The address can be displayed as a string of characters or sometimes as a QR code for easy recognition. If you want to let someone pay you in bitcoin, just send them your address and ask them to transfer funds to it.

When you start on the Bitcoin network with your new address, you can't do much until you have some bitcoin associated with it. This can happen in two ways: either you start mining bitcoin or you get someone to transfer bitcoin to you. For a private person, acquiring bitcoin by mining is not feasible anymore (more about that later). It is, therefore, necessary to get bitcoin from somewhere else, such as an exchange or selling goods.

Online exchanges allow you to deposit fiat currency, such as dollars, to be exchanged for bitcoin. The exchange will then transfer the bitcoin from one of their addresses to yours. This transaction is picked up by the Bitcoin network and captured in a block. Once this is done, you will have a balance to spend equivalent to the amount just transferred to you.

If you want to buy something or transfer it to someone else, you get their address, enter the amount you wish to transfer, and can add some text too. But note that this text will be visible to anyone on the blockchain. The transaction will then consist of the following:

- The address from which the bitcoin should be taken

- The amount

- An additional transaction fee that you might want to add to get your transaction included faster

- The address to which the bitcoin should be transferred

- Additional text

More than sending a transaction is required since anyone could send a transaction with your wallet address. For the Bitcoin network to validate the transaction, you need to sign it with the private key associated with the address. The transaction is then posted as "pending" to the Bitcoin network. The miners will then validate that the transaction is signed with the private key. Once it has been included in a block, the transaction is complete and available for all to see.

Compare this with a regular bank account, where the bank holds all data centrally, who also keeps the credentials that allow you to transfer money from the account. The bank can close access to your account or compromise your credentials to a malicious third party, who will then have access to your funds. The bank knows precisely who you are because of their Know Your Customer (KYC) processes, and they are liable to comply with court rulings to disclose your transactions or freeze funds.

With Bitcoin, no one knows who you are. There is only a nonsensical random Bitcoin address. Even though, contrary to a bank, all transactions are public, no one can connect them to you as a private person. The money is not stored centrally anywhere but rather everywhere, which means that even if a server breaks or the online exchange goes bankrupt, the money is still out there and available. Lastly, no one controls access to your funds; if you have the private key for an address, you can access all the bitcoins associated with that address. What's more, clearing a transaction is done in less than an hour compared with a few days for traditional bank transfers.

The flip side is that there are none of the guardrails and safety nets associated with regular banking. If a criminal abuses your credit card, you can dispute the transaction with the credit card company, which usually results in the successful return of the money to your account. With bitcoin, if someone gets access to your private key and transfers all the funds, there is nothing anyone can do. You cannot plead with the Bitcoin network. Similarly, if you accidentally typed the wrong address, the money would now belong to that address, and there is no way in the world you would be able to find out who that was to ask for your money back. The money would just be gone.

Shared Public Ledger

Traditional banks keep all their records of transactions secret. Indeed, that is the fundamental rule of bank secrecy, which is codified into law in many countries. When money is spent, the banks make sure an account can spend it only once through a complex interbank clearing system. Being sure that money is spent only once is a necessity for any method of exchange and part of the reason that clearing takes so long.

Hashcash had yet to solve the problem of double spending and relied on a central registry to keep track of whether a token had already been spent. The public ledger was a key innovation to solve this problem in Bitcoin. The complete privacy of the sender and receiver of a transaction allowed Bitcoin to turn the fundamental bank secrecy on its head and post all transactions in public. When all transactions are between pseudonymous wallet IDs, privacy is still ensured even if it is publicly posted.

The public ledger is one long record of all bitcoin transactions ever made. The idea of such a shared public ledger was presented by Wei Dai in his vision for B-money. From Wei Dai came the concept of a distributed ledger where all transactions were recorded for all to see. Based on this distributed ledger, account balances could be calculated at the time of a transaction, which is essentially the concept of Grigg's triple-entry accounting. These ideas were implemented for the first time in Bitcoin.

The public ledger is not just a long string of transactions that are added individually. It consists of blocks of transactions, hence the name blockchain. A block is a collection of transactions. Since the block is a record of history, it must be immutable. The hashing of the content achieves that. The block is sealed with a hash of all the transactions included in the block, so anyone can verify that the transactions contained were not altered in a later copy. It is not sufficient to just put a hash in each block because, as we saw, there is no account balance recorded anywhere. Hence, all balances require the entire record of all previous transactions involving any given Bitcoin address to validate that it has a balance to spend. If one or more blocks were missing, double spending would be possible, since the transactions in the missing block will not count toward calculating the balance of an account.

That means it is necessary for the miners validating transactions to have access to the entirety of the public ledger's history of transactions. This poses the problem of ensuring that all blocks are present and accounted for. If the block where you paid 100 bitcoins is conveniently missing from the public ledger, they would still figure as a balance you could spend in the Bitcoin system, thus allowing double spending. The solution is that each block has to include the previous block's hash, which is what makes it a chain. In this way, taking out any block from the public ledger is impossible. The previous block's hash and the transactions would not yield the same hash of subsequent blocks. Remember that a hash is a fingerprint based on all the input, so the fingerprint of the previous block is required to generate the next block's fingerprint. Nick Szabo had initially suggested this mechanism with his idea about Bitgold, but it was never implemented.

Peer-to-Peer Network

The Bitcoin network is a system of computers running the Bitcoin software and connected directly over the Internet. Transactions are published to this network for inclusion in the next block. When a new block is created, it is similarly sent to other nodes for validation and inclusion in the blockchain.

If this public ledger were maintained on a central server, it would be vulnerable to corruption and failure. This is the reason the system is distributed in a peer-to-peer network where each node on the network contains a copy of the entire public ledger. When someone wants to start mining bitcoin, it is necessary to connect to this network and download the blockchain. The network thus also works as a distributed storage system with multiple redundant copies. In this way, even if one node fails, there will be thousands of others with a copy.

Another scenario is that an alternative block is created where alternative transactions are inserted. Since most other nodes will have another version of the block, this will be rejected by the network. In the Bitcoin network, there is a built-in consensus system whereby a majority is needed to get a block accepted. The network builds on the longest chain. If the alternative block is not accepted, it will not be part of the longest chain and thereby transactions not "settled."

Given this peer-to-peer model, Bitcoin cannot be closed down by any central authority, even if regulators and pundits claim it should be. It will exist as long as there are computers that connect running the Bitcoin software. This makes Bitcoin and other similar blockchains the most resilient systems of exchange ever made. Banks can be closed down, and even central banks can disappear if a country disappears, but Bitcoin and blockchains will continue as long as anyone is dedicating computing power and network connection to running the software.

Proof of Work

The next natural question is, what do these computers running the Bitcoin software connected in a network do? The answer is that they perform the process of bitcoin mining. This process is virtually identical to the proof-of-work function of Hashcash, but how does that work in detail?

The proof-of-work principle is that performing a function should not be free. In the case of Hashcash, that function was sending emails or requests to a web server. For Bitcoin, this function is to include transactions into a block and print money, that is, bitcoin. It makes perfect sense that such a function needs to be somehow costly; otherwise, everyone would just start creating blocks to get bitcoin.

The problem is how exactly you prove that you worked on creating the block. Bundling several pending transactions together and hashing them naturally requires some work, but that is microscopic and not costly by itself. To create a cost, a cryptographic puzzle is added to this work.

Recall that a hash is essentially a number of fixed length. Bitcoin uses the SHA-256 algorithm to create a hash of all the transactions in a block. This hash is a string of 256 bits. It is represented as a hexadecimal value. The hexadecimal numbering system is what is called a base-16 encoded numbering. The base refers to how many different numbers there are in the number system. The binary system is base 2, that is, there are only two numbers: 0 and 1. The decimal system is base 10, meaning there are ten different numbers: 0 through 9. The hexadecimal system thus has 16 different numbers. Since we don't have number symbols for more than 10 in the decimal system, the additional numbers are represented with characters A through F. Since we can represent any number in a hexadecimal system with 4 bits, the resulting string in hexadecimal is 64 characters long (256/4) containing decimal numbers and letters A–F.

With this in place, let us return to the puzzle. Creating a hash without any requirements for the final string is trivial. Any hash value will do. But if we add the requirement that the resulting hash value should have one 0 in the beginning, we can no longer trivially generate the hash value. Since we know that trying the hash algorithm again won't make a difference, we have to adjust the input. We could, of course, try to add or subtract random transactions, but that is inconvenient. Instead, the Bitcoin system lets miners add a number, called a "nonce," to a block. The name refers to a "number used only once," and it is a 32-bit field. Since a hash is very sensitive to any change in input, any number in the nonce will change the resulting hash value dramatically. Therefore, the puzzle is to figure out what value to add in the nonce to make the hash of the transactions and other information in the block result in a value below the value set as the target.

As can easily be seen, there are fewer values that start with 0 than the total sum of possible hash values. If we add another zero, we further decrease the number of total acceptable hash values. In fact, with each additional 0 added, the entire solution space decreases. This means that the probability of generating the correct hash decreases with each zero added at the beginning of the target value. The consequence of this is that, on average, more tries will have to be made before a hash value that satisfies the target is found. This is the essence of mining: a cryptographic lottery. And the difficulty is proportional to the number of leading zeroes the miners must find for the resulting hash value.

One could now ask how that translates to proof of work. The answer is that each guess at the hash value requires work by a CPU. Actually, it does not have to be a CPU; you could calculate the hash yourself by hand, which has been done and takes hours. The faster the CPU, the more guesses it can try out in a period. Since there is only a reward for the first miner to arrive at a solution, time is of the essence. The faster the CPU, the more cryptographic lottery tickets you will have. The higher the difficulty, the higher the total CPU work needed to guess a correct solution.

Since Moore's law has made sure that computing power continues to expand, what was considered difficult when Satoshi wrote the Bitcoin whitepaper might be trivial today. In other words, the CPU work needed to solve a given difficulty in 2009 would be significantly cheaper today. This could undermine the proof-of-work aspect of Bitcoin, which is why the Bitcoin protocol continuously sets new targets for difficulty. For every 2,016 blocks, the difficulty is reset.

In order not to have the blocks generated too quickly and thus release all the bitcoins at once, Satoshi set the target time to create a block to an average of ten minutes. The difficulty increases if the average block generation time is less than ten minutes and decreases if the average time is more than ten minutes. The time it takes to generate the right solution depends on the total number of CPU cycles available to the Bitcoin network, or to put it simply: the total computing power of the Bitcoin network. This computing power is captured in the "hash rate" concept since the ultimate purpose is to generate a hash. The unit currently used is terahash per second, which means how many trillion hashes per second the entire network can produce. In our lottery terms, this equates to how many lottery tickets can be bought per second by all lottery participants. At the time of writing, it is around 260 million terahashes per second.

When a miner is finally successful in constructing a block, they need to get paid. This payment is newly minted bitcoins created in the new block. This number goes into the coinbase (not to be confused with the company Coinbase). The first transaction of a block is called the coinbase and is created by the miner creating the block. It contains the address of the miner and a number no greater than the current reward as defined by the Bitcoin protocol. Recall that bitcoin is disbursed on a schedule depending on how many have already been minted. Currently, the reward is 6.25 bitcoins per block.

To this reward are added the transaction fees that users included. The average transaction fee is around the equivalent of $1 but has fluctuated between $1 and $5. Transaction fees are still a minor part of the total rewards for miners. Currently, it hovers around the single-digit percentage, but at times, it has made up more than 50% of the reward. As the issuance of bitcoin decreases, it is expected that the percentage of reward derived from transaction fees will increase. After the final bitcoin, this is the only incentive for miners to continue verifying transactions and creating blocks.

What Is Bitcoin?

To summarize, Bitcoin is a system that provides access to a virtual currency, bitcoin, that anyone can start using by downloading software or using online services to create a wallet. This wallet is essentially a collection of public IDs from which transactions can be made only with the private key used to create the wallet. A transaction is made by specifying the wallet ID you want to send it to and the amount of bitcoins using the wallet software. The system is underpinned by a computer network that voluntarily provides computing resources that allows transactions to be recorded on a blockchain, which contains all transactions ever made. These computers are called miners, and they are rewarded with transaction fees and newly minted bitcoin.

As can be seen from this walk-through, Bitcoin is a complex system that brings together technological innovations from many different sources. In fact, it would be difficult to point to any particular feature that was a new invention in Bitcoin. At the same time, the complete Bitcoin solution is so radically new and innovative that one would be hard-pressed to find anything in the twenty-first century to match it. Some aspects seem unnecessarily complex and even contrived in isolation, but it is so for a reason, and when all of it is brought together, it produces a uniquely functional solution that has proved itself for more than a decade.

Bitcoin and blockchain technology are the product of technological trajectories that sometimes go back thousands of years but only now have reached a level sufficient to build a globally resilient system of exchange. These trajectories merge in often surprising and paradoxical ways. Recall that accounting, banking, and cryptography have mainly been concerned with keeping information private and secret, but Bitcoin, on the other hand, is entirely public and accessible to anyone. Another example is that virtual currencies, like all other previous currencies, have all depended on one central minting authority. Historically, the greatest challenge for currency issuers was preventing any other party from minting the currency, which is known as counterfeiting and usually carries heavy punishment with it. Again, Bitcoin turns this on its head and lets anyone mint the currency.

Bitcoin hardly drew more than a shrug and a couple of critical comments when it was created. It has been pronounced dead more times than a few times since its inception. Still, it continues to thrive as the world's most valuable virtual currency. But how did all of this come together? That is what we now turn our attention to.

CHAPTER 5

Searching for Satoshi

In modern times the identity of few people has been the object of more significant inquiry and mystery than the inventor of Bitcoin, Satoshi Nakamoto. That was, however, not in the cards when the Bitcoin whitepaper was published in October 2008. The publication was announced on the cryptography mailing list to initial critical comments by only four contributors after fizzling out within a month. By December 2008, exactly no one talked about Bitcoin, and the notion that more than a decade later the world would be intensely trying to figure out who its author Satoshi Nakamoto was seemed outlandish.

Yet, here we are, 15 years later, and some of the brightest journalists of our time writing for the most prestigious publications like *The New York Times*, *Wired*, and *Forbes* have spent countless hours trying to figure out the identity of Satoshi Nakamoto to no avail. So far, this effort has been in vain. We are still searching for Satoshi. A few people have hinted at or claimed to be Satoshi, but most have vehemently rejected being identified as him.

One could argue that this search is not important, and in the grand scheme of things, I agree, but it is still interesting. The identity of Satoshi is a modern mystery and, as such, warrants a comprehensive investigation. Since no consensus has been reached on the identity of Satoshi, it could be worthwhile to take another look. In the following, we will go through the most important investigations of the historical Satoshi, concluding that none have convincingly argued for the identity of Satoshi. In the next

© Anders Lisdorf 2023
A. Lisdorf, *Still Searching for Satoshi*, https://doi.org/10.1007/978-1-4842-9639-4_5

chapter, I will propose a new way based on the principles of historical-critical research and go through the different sources to understand what they can and cannot tell us.

Whodunnit?

It took a while before the media started to take an interest in Bitcoin and its creator. The first years were quiet. In May 2010, the first transaction took place with bitcoin when Laszlo Hanyecz bought a pizza for 10,000 bitcoins. At that time, it was only possible to get bitcoin by mining it. Bitcoin was a niche affair.

That started to change in 2011 when the first exchanges began to appear, and Bitcoin gained notoriety by connection to WikiLeaks, which wanted to accept donations in bitcoin. This brought Bitcoin to the general public's attention, and mainstream media began writing about it.

The Search Commences

The first major publication to take an interest in Bitcoin was no other than *The New Yorker* with an article written by the American writer Joshua Davis. Davis is no stranger to writing about technology and has also written technology pieces for *Wired* magazine. He is typically drawn to odd but true stories, and in 2011, the story about Bitcoin and its mysterious founder was definitely that.

The article identified several critical observations about Satoshi that would come to dominate subsequent attempts at identification: Satoshi writes in flawless British English; he was probably born in the early 1970s; he had a problem with banks, which he felt couldn't be trusted; he's a world-class programmer who programs in C++ and understands peer-to-peer programming.

The article is a journey of discovery more than a focused investigation. Davis starts with the security researcher Dan Kaminsky and then Stuart Haber of Princeton University due to three references to him in the Bitcoin whitepaper. From there, we go to the Crypto 2011 conference because Haber thinks it might be an excellent place to start. At the conference, Davis looks for people ostensibly fitting the criteria and finds one Michael Clear, a graduate student from Ireland.

Unfortunately, he did not confess to being Satoshi but brought forth another suspect, Vili Lehdonvirta, a Finnish researcher. Lehdonvirta similarly found the suggestion that he was Satoshi hilarious and even suggested that a virtual currency like Bitcoin should have a back door for governments, which completely opposes the Bitcoin whitepaper.

Ultimately Davis's quest to find Satoshi proves unsuccessful and remains just that, a quest, a great story that cemented Bitcoin as a serious object of interest. The article also pinpointed many key observations about Satoshi that any identification has to align with.

Another theme that would recur is that the people identified reject being Satoshi. This in itself is not an argument against, though, since Satoshi went to great lengths to protect his identity. The real Satoshi could not be expected to admit to any identification either. The two suggested suspects seem a little random and do not even align with Davis's observations about Satoshi: Lehdonvirta is not a native English speaker, and Clear is probably not a world-class programmer and has no experience with peer-to-peer. Both were not born at the beginning of the 1970s.

"The Bitcoin Crypto-Currency Mystery Reopened"

In response to the piece written by Joshua Davis in *The New Yorker*, professor of journalism at NYU Adam Penenberg wrote the article "The Bitcoin Crypto-Currency Mystery Reopened," which takes issue with the conclusions. He does not think Davis found the right man, although no new evidence except reiterated denials by Clear is offered, but even Davis did not seem to think Clear is Satoshi.

Penenberg uncovers another clue to Satoshi, the name: in Japanese "Satoshi" translates into "clear-thinking; quick-witted; wise." "Naka" can mean "inside" or "relationship," while "moto" is defined as "the origin; the cause; the foundation; the basis." So we have "clear-thinking" "inside" "the foundation." It is, though, not entirely clear where that leads us.

He then proceeds to question the findings of Davis that Satoshi is British by speculating that it is a red herring. But faking a different language consistently for 80,000 words for two years is incredibly difficult, if not impossible. He notes that the first mention by Satoshi was written in American and afterward turned to British, but why start with an attempt at an American accent and then switch to a British if it was not because this was easier? Penenberg fails to produce any actual argument for why Satoshi should not be British.

The method used by Penenberg is to google putatively distinct phrases from the Bitcoin whitepaper to see if there are any hits elsewhere. This produces nothing except the phrase "computationally impractical to reverse." This also shows up in a patent application with the title "Updating and Distributing Encryption Keys" from August 2008. The authors are Neal King, Charles Bry, and Vladamir Oksman. He finds that they have authored other applications that sound "Bitcoin-y" to him. The hypothesis is that these three together are behind Satoshi Nakamoto.

But recall our treatment of public key encryption in Chapter 2; "computationally impractical to reverse" is merely another way of saying trapdoor function: the central trait of the mathematical function needed in a public key cryptographic system. Further, key distribution has nothing to do with Bitcoin. King also says as much to Penenberg. Bitcoin uses public key cryptography, whose entire purpose, as we saw, was to get rid of the key distribution problem. The argument is similar to saying that the mysterious inventor of a new type of safe must be the same as the locksmith who invented a new way to update locks.

Finally, in Satoshi Nakamoto, we have a person who worked for years on proprietary intellectual property only to forfeit the intellectual property rights, which patents protect, and release it for free as open source software. How likely is it to find this person applying for a patent, which is the opposite approach to IP? Everything we know about Bitcoin is that it was made to be open and free, not closed and proprietary like a patent. Even if the authors may have superficially similar views, as Penenberg claims after viewing one author's Facebook page, their actions show the opposite.

The article thus fails to bring forth any convincing arguments or methodical rigor to the investigation of the identity of Satoshi.

The Search Continues

It seems that the search for Satoshi subsided after the initial interest, not because it was believed that any of the identifications were correct, though. In 2013 speculation started again. Ted Nelson, considered one of the Internet's founding fathers, released a video where he identified Satoshi Nakamoto as the reclusive Japanese mathematician Shinichi Mochizuki. There was no argument as to why that would be, other than Mochizuki being a genius who had once before dropped a proof on the Internet and left all discussion of it. While Nelson speculates his English must be good since he moved to the United States at age five, it does not answer how he had learned to command British English. There is similarly no indication that he had any interest in cryptography or any abilities to program.

In another article, Alec Liu reviews the list of suspects and adds Gavin Andresen, who took over the reins of developing Bitcoin from Satoshi in 2010. Also, Jed McCaleb, the co-founder of mtgox, was identified since he helped build the first successful exchange, which was incorporated in Japan. The conclusion was that no really good fit had been found. One interesting takeaway from the article was that Satoshi's coding style seems to have been something other than that of a professional developer, but rather an academic.

Two Israeli computer scientists, Dorit Ron and Adi Shamir, published a paper analyzing the Bitcoin blockchain and noticed a financial connection between the Bitcoin creator and Ross Ulbricht, the creator of the Silk Road dark net market for illicit goods and services. Ulbricht denied it through his attorney, and the researchers later retracted the finding.

The *Newsweek* Story

In an apparent bombshell in *Newsweek* in 2014, the identity of Satoshi Nakamoto was revealed to be a man whose name is Dorian Prentice Satoshi Nakamoto by investigative reporter Leah McGrath Goodman: "Tacitly acknowledging his role in the Bitcoin project, he looks down, staring at the pavement and categorically refuses to answer questions."

"I am no longer involved in that, and I cannot discuss it," he says, dismissing all further queries with a swat of his left hand. "It's been turned over to other people. They are in charge of it now. I no longer have any connection."

Had Satoshi finally been found? Goodman started her two-month investigation from another angle, that Satoshi Nakamoto is not a pseudonym but his real name, and tried to find someone by that name. She succeeded and found a Japanese-American man named Dorian Nakamoto living in Temple City outside Los Angeles, California.

While certain aspects of Satoshi Nakamoto align, such as a distrust of government and banks, most others seem not to. Most important is his wife's assessment of his English skills: "I would not say he writes flawless English. He will pick up words and mix the spellings." None of this is evident in the writings we know of Satoshi Nakamoto.

The question is then, why, or what was he admitting to when he said that he was no longer involved? Dorian Nakamoto had worked on military projects earlier in his career. Given his limited understanding of English, he seems to have thought that the reporter was referring to this. Curiously following this incident, Satoshi Nakamoto apparently returned to public writing that he was not Dorian Nakamoto on the P2P forum site.

Nakamoto's Neighbor

Forbes, in another attempt to identify Satoshi, had requested a comparison of all the previously identified suspects with that of Satoshi Nakamoto and found that the one that most resembled Satoshi was Clear, whom Joshua Davis had mentioned. Andy Greenberg, at the time a writer for *Forbes*, didn't feel the identification of Satoshi as Dorian Nakamoto held up because of the language and asked to include his writings in the analysis, which showed that Dorian Nakamoto was a worse match than Clear.

Spurred by a tip about the coincidence that Hal Finney also lived in the comparatively small community of Temple City, Greenberg started investigating whether he might be Satoshi. As we saw earlier, Finney was a central figure in cryptography in general and virtual currencies in particular. Even if Dorian Nakamoto was not Satoshi Nakamoto, it might have been Hal Finney taking his name since they lived only 1.6 miles from each other.

Finney denied both that Dorian Nakamoto could have been the inventor and any knowledge about him and showed Greenberg the email communication with Nakamoto (which was compared against the writings of the real Satoshi Nakamoto to verify it) and the first transactions, where Satoshi sent ten bitcoins to Finney. The timestamps on the emails lined up with these transactions. He concludes, "The notion that Finney alone might have set up the two accounts and created a fake conversation with himself to throw off snoops like me, long before Bitcoin had any measurable value, seemed preposterous."

A New Suspect Appears

Another suspect emerged around the same time, one that, like Hal Finney, had been deeply involved in virtual currencies and the cypherpunks since the beginning: Nick Szabo. He had been an early employee in the first successful virtual currency company, DigiCash, and had continued this interest throughout. Around the end of 2003, a blogger calling themself Skye Grey posted two blog posts that argued that Nick Szabo was the inventor of Bitcoin. The story was picked up by TechCrunch, which interviewed Skye Grey.

The argument was made primarily from an analysis of similarities between the Bitcoin whitepaper and writings by Nick Szabo. Much significance was placed on Szabo's blog post describing his idea of Bitgold, even though it was barely a thousand words and expounded many of the ideas that others like Wei Dai and Adam Back had already suggested.

The methodology was a putatively forensic analysis of characteristic phrases in the Bitcoin whitepaper, using a seemingly homemade method of looking at textual "tics," that is, identifying tells of style in the Bitcoin whitepaper and comparing those with Nick Szabo. Grey determines some content-neutral terms: repeated use of "of course" without isolating commas, the expression "can be characterized," use of "for our purposes" when describing hypotheses, starting sentences with "It should be noted," etc. These seem like fairly common expressions and standard academic language. It seems that Grey fails to argue for their distinctiveness.

There are also "content-bearing" terms like "timestamp server," central in the Bitcoin paper, "trusted third party," "cryptographic proof," "digital signatures," and repeated use of "timestamp" as a verb," but these are, as we have seen, similarly quite regular expressions in cryptography and pervade debates on the cryptography mailing list. It seems that the simpler explanation is that Satoshi and Szabo both belong to the same linguistic subcommunity of academics specializing in cryptography.

The same method was used later in 2014 in a study by Aston University Institute for Forensic Linguistics headed by lecturer Jack Grieve and 40 of his final-year students. They seem to have followed the same method and compared the Bitcoin whitepaper to 11 other suspects. It was, unfortunately, never published, so it is not possible to check or replicate the findings or see why there was no comparison to the 80,000 other words Satoshi wrote. It would also have been interesting to understand how a forensic analysis can gloss over the glaring difference between American (written by Szabo) and British English (written by Satoshi).

Evidence Builds

Journalist Dominic Frisby similarly singled out Nick Szabo in his 2014 book *Bitcoin: The Future of Money?* Frisby provides a lengthy exposition and unveils other circumstantial evidence, such as the fact that he has been working in this area for most of his life and has written about similar ideas many years in advance. Szabo also seems to have had a vacant period before Bitcoin was produced and asked for help coding a project. Four months later, the site bitcoin.org. was registered, and Szabo was updating his blog posts about his related Bitgold idea.

As for the linguistic evidence, Frisby uses the dubious and unpublished postulates by Skye Grey and the Aston University student report. Frisby himself has excellent insight into the writings of Satoshi and claims that he is very consistent in his British spellings but finds a handful of Americanisms. From this, he concludes that the author must be American. Still, would a handful of Americanisms in a consistently well-formed British English not instead indicate a Brit who had some exposure to America than an American with exposure to Great Britain? That seems to be a more parsimonious explanation.

A final observation concerns the coding of Bitcoin. There is no evidence that Szabo ever coded in C++. There are examples of his coding in other languages, which begs the question of why he would choose C++. Curiously, Frisby lets this fact slip easily after having dismissed almost everyone else just because they did not like C++.

While Frisby must be commended for some of the most comprehensive research to date and for bringing a substantial amount of new circumstantial evidence to light, it is hard to dismiss the two really hard pieces of evidence: the linguistic and the code. The more straightforward explanation is still that Satoshi is a Native British English speaker with well-documented coding skills in C++. Neither fits Szabo even if he had the ideas, motive, and opportunity to create Bitcoin.

Nathaniel Popper, who wrote a similarly thorough work released the following year, *Digital Gold: Bitcoin and the Inside Story of the Misfits and Millionaires Trying to Reinvent Money*, joined Frisby in identifying Szabo as Satoshi. He managed to speak to the otherwise reclusive Szabo privately, where Szabo denied being Satoshi. Popper reiterates the previous points made by Frisby and adds a few more pieces of circumstantial evidence but similarly neglects to address the central issue of language and the ability to code in C++.

The Plot Thickens

In 2015 *Wired* ran a piece that it subsequently retracted, claiming that the Australian Craig Steven Wright was Satoshi Nakamoto. Wright himself claimed to be Satoshi and sent the documents, first to security researcher Gwern Branwen and then to *Wired*. The documents turned out to be an elaborate hoax. Wright later continued to claim that he was Satoshi and together with the deceased Dave Kleiman developed Bitcoin.

He even claimed to be able to prove it by having keys that could be linked to Satoshi, but in the end, they never checked out, and Wright claimed that he didn't want to proceed to provide the evidence needed.

He even had some senior Bitcoin people like Gavin Andresen convinced for a short while, but since no cryptographic proof was provided, the claims could not be verified.

In 2019 *Wired* had another go at identifying Satoshi that was curiously connected to Craig Wright. Writer and journalist Evan Ratliff had spent five years tracking the South African global criminal mastermind Paul Calder Le Roux, who also happened to be a programmer. This research resulted in a 400-page book about Le Roux. Through the process, Ratliff had several times come across circumstantial evidence that could indicate Le Roux was Satoshi, but he had put it away again.

That started to change after messages came in about a multibillion-dollar lawsuit in Florida. The defendant in the case was none other than Craig Wright, the self-proclaimed Satoshi. It was brought by Ira Kleiman, the brother of a deceased business partner of Wright, Dave Kleiman. Ira Kleiman asserted that Wright and Kleiman had mined hundreds of thousands of bitcoins together and that Wright transferred them to himself. The lawyers representing Wright filed a motion to seal his responses to specific questions because it would endanger himself and other persons as well as national security. These persons and footnotes were redacted except one that his lawyers had overlooked. It was a footnote containing links to a news article and a Wikipedia article about…Paul Calder Le Roux!

Ratliff returned to his notes and started to re-examine the circumstantial evidence he had brushed away and found more. Here is a selection: Le Roux knew C++ and had already, in the 1990s, developed a disk encryption tool that was later open-sourced. He was about the age that collaborators thought Satoshi was (born in 1975); being an international drug lord, he had more motive than anyone and a natural hatred for banks; he got a Congolese diplomatic passport with the name Paul Solotshi Calder Le Roux. This was two weeks before he first contacted Adam Back under the name Satoshi. Even the timing of Satoshi's disappearance aligns with his arrest in 2012.

So far, Ratliff's analysis has followed the model of previous identifications of Satoshi, but he takes a step back and evaluates the evidence against Le Roux: he was not an academic, and on a more philosophical note, Le Roux was not against spam as Satoshi was, since he ran one of the most significant spam operations on the planet. Eventually, this led Ratliff to the following realization:

> *Because Le Roux so clearly could be Satoshi, he was therefore more likely to be. Missing from that equation was a calculation of all possible people who could also be Satoshi. There were untold numbers of programmers who were adept at C++ and hated government, who felt a responsibility to credit other coders and used the phrase "encryption for the masses," who had reasons to stay anonymous and expressed some interest in digital currencies. To prove anything about Le Roux via my technique, I'd have to disprove dozens, perhaps hundreds, of equally likely candidates.*

Full Circle

We have come full circle, back to where we started with no clue as to who Satoshi is or how to find out. Ratliff's piece seems to be emblematic of all previous investigations we have considered: The journalist, for they were all written by journalists, for one reason or another, intuits a possible suspect and starts collecting evidence. The evidence for is attributed greater significance than the evidence against. This is also called cherry-picking facts. All previous investigations have proceeded from a suspect to selecting evidence with no principled inquiry but plenty of assumptions and subjective assessments. Ratliff deserves respect since he as the first saw clearly that this approach was not sufficient to provide evidence of who Satoshi is. Consequently, even after more than a decade of intense scrutiny, we are still searching for Satoshi.

It is time that the search for Satoshi was turned around and started from a basis of principles derived from academic historical inquiry rather than ad hoc fact fitting. The next chapter will therefore lay a foundation for a more structured investigation into what we can say about Satoshi and how we can identify him.

CHAPTER 6

Profiling Satoshi

The Historical Basis for Satoshi

To restart the search for Satoshi on a more solid basis, we have to go through a sequence of steps in a principled way. The first step is to realize that this is a historical problem and should be analyzed and investigated as we would any other kind of historical problem. Through the aid of the discipline of modern historiographical research, we can approach the problem in a more principled way.

Before the nineteenth century, Western history was characterized by two different traditions of writing history, according to Georg G. Iggers, a specialist in the nature of history and historiography. One was learned and antiquarian focusing on cataloging facts, and the other was essentially literary, where the focus was on the story told. This changed only when the modern discipline of history emerged from German universities in the nineteenth century.

The primary force in this change was the German historian Leopold von Ranke who became a professor of history at the University of Berlin in 1825, a post he held for 50 years. In his first book, *Histories of the Latin and Teutonic Nations from 1494 to 1514* from 1824, he set the new direction with one sentence that essentially became the slogan for modern history, namely, that the purpose of the historian was to show how it really was ("wie es eigentlich gewesen ist"). This might seem self-evident today, but contrasted with contemporary history writing where the focus was on

© Anders Lisdorf 2023
A. Lisdorf, *Still Searching for Satoshi*, https://doi.org/10.1007/978-1-4842-9639-4_6

telling an engaging narrative, von Ranke used a more significant variety of sources than his contemporaries and limited himself to only talk about what he could base on the sources, not imagination and conjectures.

From this grew the practice of source criticism that has been particularly elaborated in the German and Scandinavian schools of historiography. The purpose of source criticism is to ensure that we write history as it was. Let us look at some of the common principles for source criticism that we will use as guidance for our search for Satoshi.

Primary and Secondary Sources

One of the key insights of Leopold von Ranke was that there is a significant difference between primary and secondary sources. Primary sources give direct access to the historical issue under investigation, that is, first-hand information. These include diaries, transcripts, correspondence, and some scholarly articles.

Secondary sources provide second-hand information and thus relate information about the historical issue to the reader through an intermediary. These contain an interpretation and selection of the original source material. Examples are biographies, commentaries, reviews, and journalistic and review articles.

Von Ranke emphasized primary sources almost to the point where he dismissed the utility of secondary sources altogether. Primary sources do indeed bring us closer to how it really was, and there is good reason always to prioritize primary sources in a historical investigation. Sometimes it may be helpful to use secondary sources where no primary sources exist while taking great care to understand and account for the tendency of the source, which we will get back to shortly.

For Bitcoin, the primary sources are those related directly to Satoshi and the development of Bitcoin—all writings by Satoshi, the whitepaper, correspondence with collaborators, and the code. Secondary sources are interviews and articles written about Bitcoin. We will prefer the first group of sources.

Relic and Narrative

Another essential distinction lies in how you use a source. A common distinction is made between what is called a relic and a narrative. The narrative is the easiest to understand. It tells us about something that happened. On the other hand, a relic tells us something about the creator of the source at the time it was created. A diary from a sailor on Captain Cook's ship, the *HMS Resolution*, can be a relic that can tell us about sailors' language and educational level, the state of mind, and the values and attitude of the sailor at the time of writing. It can also be a narrative about the first encounter by Europeans with Hawaiians. Using a source as a relic is more credible than as a narrative since narratives have biases. Relics don't lie, but narratives can.

In the case of Bitcoin, we can use the writings of Satoshi as relics saying something about his language, education, attitudes, style, and time of writing. We can use interviews of collaborators as narratives about the creation of Bitcoin and Satoshi's person.

Tendency of the Source

Interpreting a source always has to account for the tendency or bias of the source. What is the interest of the author of the source? And how does that fit the information conveyed by the source? An excerpt from the ship log of Captain Cook's *HMS Resolution* relating to the death of Captain Cook at the hands of the Hawaiians is bound to be biased toward portraying the civilized manner in which the Europeans thought themselves to have engaged the Hawaiians. The portrayal of the actions of the Hawaiians as savage will thus be biased and cannot be taken at face value. To use any source, we have to be clear about the author's interest before we start using it as evidence for anything. This also means that information that is neutral in relation to the bias can be used. That is information the author can be said to have no natural reason to lie about. This is often used in historical accounts. Information going against the bias will therefore acquire even more value. Using information from a source that follows its bias has little, if any, value. For example, an interview with someone suspected of being Satoshi is biased toward not revealing evidence of the person being Satoshi since Satoshi does not want to be identified. Any sources of this type consequently have no value.

Closeness to the Event

A source's value increases with its closeness to the event. A diary entry written aboard the *HMS Resolution* in Hawaii at the same time as Captain Cook's encounter with the Hawaiians is much more valuable than an autobiography by a sailor related 50 years later.

Even though the advent of Bitcoin is a relatively recent event and therefore fairly close, the principle of closeness to the event is still important. Sources that are closer to the creation of Bitcoin and Satoshi, therefore, have preference to later interviews, even if they are with key people.

Independent Confirmation

The last significant principle has to do with corroboration. The more independent sources can confirm a state of affairs, the better. Having only a single account, even if it is of high quality, can be dangerous to rely on. For any fact, we should always find independent confirmation from other sources.

This means that we should look at other ways to get an independent confirmation for each fact we identify. Much previous investigation has relied too much on single observations like a single comment or proximity in time of events. That might lead to spurious conclusions. It may not always be possible, but without corroborating evidence, any claim is weak.

Parsimony

The general scientific principle of parsimony should be added to these historical principles of source criticism. It is the principle that entities used for an explanation should not be multiplied beyond what is necessary. We have already seen examples of such in the previous attempts at the identification of Satoshi. Several authors end up suggesting two or more persons since one only fits some of the facts. This is an unnecessary multiplication of entities beyond what is necessary.

It is also known as Occam's razor. This principle requires that comparing competing hypotheses, the one with the fewest assumptions must be preferred. Another way is to say that given multiple competing theories, it should be the simplest explanation that is chosen. This, of course, does not guarantee that we arrive at the truth, but such is the nature of scientific work. It does, however, increase the likelihood of finding the truth vastly. The only alternative is to cherry-pick facts and go down the road of conspiracy theories, where we invent elaborate theories in support of our claims as we explain away conflicting evidence, if we even address it.

Ad Fontes: What Can the Sources Tell Us?

With the principles in place, let us consider the different groups of sources pertaining to the creation of Bitcoin and its creator. One general observation is that sources that can be attributed to Satoshi are primary sources and therefore take precedence over all other sources.

A short note about the use of the male pronoun in connection with Satoshi: It is not impossible that Satoshi is a woman, but in a field like cryptography where women number in the single-digit percentage, the simplest assumption before we start looking at actual evidence is that the author is a man. We will return to this question later.

The Bitcoin Whitepaper

The Bitcoin whitepaper is the most important single source for identifying Satoshi. It is a primary source that can give us direct access to the person behind Satoshi Nakamoto since he wrote it. Consequently, it can tell us a great deal about him, his style, his values, and his preferences. The first thing to notice is that it is written in fluent academic British English.

It is formatted according to the guidelines of the IEEE publishing standard. There are many competing standards in academic publishing, and each differs a little bit. The author must consequently have submitted at least one article using the IEEE guidelines, which are quite widely used in computer science.

Satoshi must therefore have a history as an academic. He need not be employed full-time as such, but as a minimum, he has participated in the preparation of an academic paper in the field of computer science at some point.

Correspondence

Satoshi corresponded a great deal in different public forums about Bitcoin. Some put the volume at more than 80,000 words. This is a sizeable collection. These forum posts are also primary sources that can be used as relics. We will, for example, see that the times of writing are essential for identifying Satoshi. The correspondences are also an important source to be used as the simplest assumption again is that Satoshi is not communicating with himself in public. The forum posts can also tell us something about the history and motives behind the creation.

There is another group of sources relating to correspondence with Satoshi: emails. These were released to the public much later when it was clear that Bitcoin was a significant thing. There are also comments about what Satoshi said in those emails. These are more dubious on technical grounds since email data can easily be changed. They are also further removed from the event than the forum posts and can, therefore, not be considered as valuable sources.

Technical Forensic Evidence

The Bitcoin code is a primary source and shows the coding style of Satoshi. As such it is a crucial piece of evidence since anyone considered a possible match for Satoshi must have the skills to write the original Bitcoin code.

The blockchain in itself can also be used as a source. As we will see, much has been made of the first block in which a quote was embedded. This is an example of evidence that is impossible to fake, which may tell us something about the person behind Satoshi.

There are other technical sources, such as the bitcoin.org web page. Here we can see through the Internet archive what was displayed at different times. Satoshi's known email addresses may also hold clues.

Interviews

A large body of evidence also exists in later interviews made with key actors in the formative period of Bitcoin. These are all secondary sources and can be used primarily as corroborating evidence. They are further removed in time and will depend on memory and later historical developments. They have virtually no value in themselves and only when they relate something that cannot be learned from primary sources.

The Sources and Satoshi

These few practical principles for approaching the sources will provide us with a guide to analyzing the problem at hand. We saw that the sources can be grouped into four groups.

- The key source: The Bitcoin whitepaper

- Correspondence between Satoshi and collaborators on public forums

- Technical forensic evidence

- Later interviews with people close to Satoshi and the beginning of Bitcoin

With a firmer grasp on the nature of the sources, we are in a better position to start searching for Satoshi. We will give precedence to the primary sources written by Satoshi himself and especially to facts that are impossible or hard to fake, such as technical forensic evidence. Other secondary sources can be used as corroborating evidence and help fill in the blanks. In the following, we will construct a profile of what we can know about the historical person behind Satoshi.

Building a Profile of Satoshi

Based on our knowledge of the sources, we can now start to investigate what we know about the historical Satoshi. In the following, we will build a profile based on what we can learn about him from the sources. But before we do that, it would be worthwhile to reflect on the very source of the mystery of Satoshi, that is, why does he use a pseudonym? To understand that, we must go back to when Satoshi published his ideas. That was at a time when a few high-profile cases involving virtual currencies had seen the founders get into serious legal problems. In 2007, the FBI raided Bernard von NotHaus's Liberty dollar on suspicion of money laundering, mail fraud, wire fraud, and counterfeiting. Charges had not yet been filed, but in another virtual currency crackdown, the e-gold founders had entered a plea agreement and pleaded guilty to the operation of an unlicensed money-transmitting business and conspiracy to engage in money laundering activity. There was no reason to assume that the US authorities would think any differently about a project like Bitcoin.

Assumptions

Today creators of virtual currencies are not prosecuted, and more transparent regulation exists that makes it less likely that the creator of Bitcoin would end up in legal trouble. So why does he not step forward? The immense success of Bitcoin only adds to the original concern. The historical person behind the Satoshi pseudonym sits on more than a million bitcoins, which amount to billions of dollars. Coming forward would best-case make it challenging to live a quiet private life and worst-case bring about severe threats to himself and his family.

There is, therefore, every reason to expect that, whoever the person behind Satoshi is, he will not be likely to admit it. On the other hand, the reverse does not follow, as some people assume that the denial of being Satoshi is evidence that the person is Satoshi. In the following, a couple of assumptions are made that will guide the analysis. I believe any identification of the historical person behind Satoshi must fulfill these assumptions.

The Assumption of Unity

The first is the assumption of unity, which is that all writings attributed to Satoshi are authored by the same author. That means we assume that the code was written by the same person who wrote the whitepaper, the Bitcoin website, the emails on the cryptography mailing list, and the various forum posts signed by Satoshi Nakamoto.

The Assumption of Singularity

The second assumption is the assumption of singularity; contrary to some earlier attempts, I don't see any reason to assume that this is not just one person. As we saw earlier, the theory that multiple people are behind Satoshi has been used to compensate for the inability to fit all facts into one individual. But as an explanatory approach, this is not advisable. We want to arrive at the simplest possible explanation. Allowing for multiple people to make up Satoshi, first of all, raises the question of why a group of people would take the unprecedented step to write as one person rather than multiple individual pseudonyms and opens for pure fantasy where any person can be picked to fit any fact. While it could be true, it is not a principled analytic way to proceed.

The Assumption of Normalcy

The third assumption is the assumption of normalcy. It has more to do with what kind of conversation we can have about Satoshi. Different varieties of conspiracy theories could be proposed where individual pieces of evidence are assumed to be deceitfully planted by Satoshi or other nefarious actors behind the scenes. Such scenarios cannot be ruled out since they are within the realm of the theoretically possible; the NSA and FBI could have assigned a division to create Bitcoin to track criminal transactions, or a clandestine circle of pedophiles could have orchestrated the creation of Bitcoin to be able to ease the trafficking of minors without government scrutiny. These theories could be true, like the existence of gnomes and the earth being flat, but they are outside the realm of serious discussion and rely only on *a priori* faith and systematically disregard facts and arguments.

In contrast to that approach, I will revert to an assumption of normalcy in human behavior. When Bitcoin was created, the person could not have foreseen that it would become this big, especially given the track record of earlier virtual currencies. So elaborate schemes with mailing oneself from a pseudonymous account and commenting on one's postings made under the pseudonym to create a cover or having every post translated or copyedited by a British English speaker seem excessive and outside normal human behavior. The historical Satoshi is assumed to have engaged with the Bitcoin community, at least initially, only under the pseudonym Satoshi Nakamoto and written in the language that was natural for him. He expressed only views that he held himself.

I don't intend to engage in speculation based on circumstantial evidence. I will rely only on the simplest possible explanation, which is that Satoshi is just one person writing in his native tongue to different people about his ecash project, which he programmed himself. That project came to be known as Bitcoin.

Profiling Nakamoto

Let's see what we can say based on the evidence at hand. Although we have a vast corpus of texts, it is almost entirely focused on technical details. Virtually no personal clues are given, and very little else is explicitly stated that can be used to create a detailed picture of the person behind Satoshi Nakamoto.

Gender

There is no definite indication of gender, but the field of modern cryptography and virtual currencies is almost exclusively a male field. I have at least not been able to identify more than a few women in this field. One exception is Cynthia Dwork. Historically it is a different case since a significant number of women worked in cryptology around World War II.

Males similarly dominate the cryptography mailing list. Around the time when Satoshi worked, I could only find Lynn Wheeler and Sandy Harris as examples of women active on the list. These are, of course, not necessarily their correct names. All identities that I could verify are male.

Age

On the P2P Foundation forum, Satoshi lists his birth date as April 5, 1975. There is no reason to believe that date given that Satoshi was obsessed with anonymity. Like the name, some effort has been made to extract symbolism from this date. April 5, 1933, was the day American president Franklin D. Roosevelt signed executive order 6102 forbidding ownership of gold coins, bullions, and certificates. This was a significant event for many libertarians interested in virtual currency. The year 1975 was the year when it again became legal to own gold in the United States. Satoshi is not particularly preoccupied with gold, however. He mentions gold only twice in the sources we have. The first time is in the Bitcoin whitepaper, where he uses gold mining to explain the concept of Bitcoin mining. The other place is in reference to e-gold, the company that was closed by the FBI.

Still, it is not an unlikely explanation for the choice of the particular date April 5, 1975, but there are other indications that this date is probably pretty close. He might be slightly older but not much younger.

Close collaborators of Satoshi, like Gavin Andresen, who took over Bitcoin development after Satoshi, also indicate that he was probably around that age. The choice of C++ could be an indication. C++ first appeared in 1985 and was a natural choice for someone studying at the start of the 1990s. At that time, it was the most popular object-oriented language. Hal Finney notes the following about Satoshi's use of C++ in an interview with Andy Greenberg from 2014: "Satoshi was a master of the intricacies, and I've only seen this in young programmers. It seems hard to master C++ if you didn't learn it while you're young."

Java was created in 1995 and would have been a natural choice if Satoshi had been educated at the end of the 1990s. If Satoshi had been older and educated in the 1970s or 1980s, the language of choice might have been C, Fortran, or Pascal. The choice of C++ is consistent with education starting around 1990, which would put the birth date between 1970 and 1975. Anyone can learn C++, but the simplest explanation is that this language was the one Satoshi was most comfortable with when he started on the Bitcoin project and that would be the language he learned during his formative years.

Geography

There is, fortunately, better evidence to pinpoint the location of Satoshi. In one of the most thorough investigations of the forensic evidence, Doncho Karaivanov provides convincing proof that Satoshi must have been based in the United Kingdom, probably in London.

Plotting the 742 known timestamps of the time Satoshi was active when he posted to forums, sent emails, and committed code to SourceForge provides a clear picture of his activity pattern. First, it eliminates Japan and Australia as candidate countries. He would have to have lived like a vampire, never working during the day, only at night, if he had worked out of Australia or Japan. The three other time zones that have been suggested, GMT (UK/Europe), Eastern Time (east coast of the United States), or Pacific Time (west coast of the United States), are all possible.

The article based on the timestamp data concludes: "At first glance, all three locations seem plausible. In London, he is a night owl, working until the early hours of the morning and sleeping until noon. On the east coast, he works up until the end of the day and then sleeps until early morning. On the west coast, he is an early bird, going to bed early in the night, but also waking up very early. Looking at this data alone, we cannot determine, beyond a reasonable doubt, which time zone Satoshi lived in."

The proof that tilts the identification toward London turns out to be embedded in the Bitcoin blockchain. In the so-called Genesis block, the first block created on January 3, there is embedded the following message: "Chancellor on brink of second bailout for banks." This appeared on the front page of *The Times* of London newspaper print edition on January 3, 2009. *The Times* circulated in all of Britain, but in 2008, 43% of its readership came from London. There was also a US edition, but it had different content than the British edition.

The Times also had an Internet site, which could have been perused if Satoshi had lived in one of the other two time zones, but the headline in the Internet edition was slightly different: "Chancellor Alistair Darling on brink of second bailout for banks." It must be said that there were pictures available of covers on the website where Satoshi could have seen the cover, but this was under the menu "Our Papers" furthest to the right next to the "Archive" menu. This is an odd thing to click if you were looking for daily news. There are other ways too that this headline could have been seen: Reuters provided a summary of the article that featured the same headline as the print edition. This is similarly a peculiar way to read your news. Therefore, the simplest explanation is that Satoshi subscribed to *The Times* and saw the print edition's front page on January 3.

There is evidence that muddles this picture of Satoshi residing in London. The timestamp in the metadata of the first draft of the Bitcoin whitepaper PDF shows the time zone as UTC-7. Daylight savings time puts the location in the Pacific time zone. It is not immediately clear what the significance of this is, but another interesting clue from forensic evidence might place Satoshi in California later in January 2009. Dominic Frisby mentions the fact that Hal Finney posted a log of debugging information in the beginning when Satoshi and Finney were the only ones running Bitcoin. This log reveals that Satoshi's machine was running in California at that time. That would be after the Genesis block of January 3 and the launch of Bitcoin on January 8 when Hal Finney had started to run Bitcoin.

I was not able to verify this, and the logs that Frisby refers to are not to be found on the links provided. Still, it might be possible that Satoshi was visiting California. Since he could be an academic, he could be there at one of California's famous universities for research purposes or a conference. The second version of the Bitcoin whitepaper PDF saved on March 24, 2009, has metadata with UTC-6, which is Mountain Time, and consequently locates Satoshi's computer in New Mexico, Utah, Arizona, or similar. Maybe he was on a sabbatical, traveling? Perhaps someone else generated the PDFs? Who knows? Either way, these isolated pieces do not invalidate the vast majority of evidence placing Satoshi in London or at least the United Kingdom.

If we look at the two other candidate time zones, they indicate that Satoshi was working on Bitcoin during the workday over a three-year period. This would mean that he was making Bitcoin full-time. He would therefore have to have enough funds saved to live for three years. That would be a lot of money. Where did he get this? His peers judge the code not to be from a professional programmer. Another admittedly very circumstantial piece of forensic evidence indicates that his computer was small. In a discussion on Bitcoin Talk, the user MoonShadow writes that it would take hours between blocks when only Satoshi was mining at a time when the difficulty was minimal. This indicates that the computer wasn't particularly powerful. It would be curious if you saved up to build a system for three years and did not have money for a powerful computer. I think it is more probable that Satoshi had a full-time job and worked afternoons and nights on Bitcoin as a hobby project, which again aligns better with the time zone data that would have him writing evenings and nights in GMT.

In conclusion, we can say that it is highly unlikely that Satoshi was based in Japan or Australia, possible but unlikely that he was in the US Eastern or Pacific time zone, and highly likely that he was based in the GMT time zone, probably in London or elsewhere in the United Kingdom.

Nationality

The name is unmistakably Japanese, and some have tried to extract meaning from it. *Satoshi* means something like "clear-thinking, quick-witted," and *Nakamoto* means central origin, someone who lives in the middle. I am not sure how that is to be interpreted. It is not a rare name: there are several Satoshi Nakamotos in the United States, and the website transfermarkt.com, which lists the value of soccer players in the world, knows of no less than 66 professional players with the last name Nakamoto and 115 with the first name Satoshi. The name, therefore, seems common enough that even someone who did not know what it means and with no detailed knowledge of the Japanese language and culture could have chosen it as a pseudonym. There is only one other reference that ties Satoshi to Japan, which is the use of the email address satoshi@anonymousspeech.com. The website anonymousspeech.com was a company based in Tokyo, Japan. But Satoshi also used other mail services known for their anonymity like vistomail.com and gmx.com that were based in Europe.

There is consensus that Satoshi writes in almost perfect British English, indicating that his nationality is to be found in the British Commonwealth, probably the United Kingdom. Alternatively, it could be Australia, New Zealand, or South Africa, but no distinguishing phrases or terms used in these countries have been identified.

It is uncontroversial that Satoshi writes in British English consistently. He uses British words like "bloody," -ou- instead of the American -o- as in "labour," and the British -ise- instead of the American -ize-. There are occasional uses of American words, but such is the case for almost any language of the world today. It would probably require years of training, as done in counterintelligence services, to be able to convincingly and consistently fake a foreign language as Satoshi would have to if he were not a British native speaker. As has been stated earlier, Satoshi is from the

British Commonwealth; realistically, that would be the United Kingdom, Australia, New Zealand, or South Africa. Given the likely location in the United Kingdom, it is therefore highly likely that he was British.

Education and Work

Nothing much is known with certainty about the education of Satoshi. It seems clear that he had higher education in the field of mathematics or computer science, judging from the references in the Bitcoin whitepaper. It is difficult to say precisely what field or the highest level, but it seems to be either a master's or PhD. He had a particular interest in cryptography since he was on the cryptography mailing list and had a deep knowledge of specific areas. He was also interested in peer-to-peer computing, evidenced by his participation in the P2P Foundation forum.

The Bitcoin whitepaper shows a firm grasp on academic writing, structure, and citation standards. It is not unreasonable to assume that he has published at least one article before. Gavin Andresen, who took over Bitcoin development after Satoshi left, believes his code was not from a professional coder. He might have worked as an academic, researcher, or consultant in the field of security.

Some have speculated that he worked in banking or had an education in finance, but this is difficult to ascertain since most of what he produced was focused on working out the technical details. He does mention the economy and banking a few times, but these quotes do not seem to be anything more than standard libertarian talking points that you can read from anyone on the cryptography mailing list: banks are bad, fractional banking is bad and they irresponsibly lend out money creating credit bubbles, central banks create inflation, etc. There is the occasional citation of Austrian economists, but when the user xc on July 27, 2010, posts a fairly deep piece of monetary theory referencing Mises and Rothbard about money regression, the emergence of money, and how Bitcoin satisfies the requirements, Satoshi doesn't seem to understand. As a response, he ventures into an odd thought experiment of a scarce metal with no real practical value and the possibility to transport it over a communications channel. He latches on to the property of scarcity, which is entirely beside the point of the post by xc; he offers no references and reverts to "I think." This passage contrasts to his writings on cryptography or technology, where Satoshi is much more confident. I, therefore, find it unlikely that Satoshi had any formal education above under graduate courses or work experience related to finance or the economy.

Values

Satoshi's values lean libertarian and anti-government, but not excessively so, which is seen from the incident at the end of December 2010 where it was suggested that WikiLeaks should start using bitcoins. Other users in the Bitcoin Talk forum argued for this, but Satoshi was relatively firmly against it. The argument is that it would bring unwanted attention.

As already noted, he has a problem with central banks because they recklessly print money. Banks are also bad because they will cooperate with the government and compromise your privacy. They also charge too much to supply their services, which is why keeping transactions free is something he continuously fights for.

There are no radical libertarian viewpoints, such as the abolition of all government authority or the complete dismantling of government regulation of trade with illicit substances, as some later proponents of Bitcoin have assumed. There is no evidence that his motivation was to facilitate drug trading, money laundering, or any other illicit type of exchange. Indeed when he gives examples of how he sees Bitcoin being used, they appear somewhat pedestrian. In a forum post on September 23, 2010, he writes, "Bitcoin would be convenient for people who don't have a credit card or don't want to use the cards they have, either don't want the spouse to see it on the bill or don't trust their number to porn guys or afraid of recurring billing."

In a reply to Dustin Trammell on January 17, 2009, the very beginning of Bitcoin, he imagines Bitcoin as variously: reward points, donation tokens, in-game currency, or micropayment for adult sites. Other potential applications Satoshi envisioned could be subscription sites and email proof of work. The last point is directly taken from Hashcash, but the use for reward points had also already been around since the turn of the millennium as evidenced by Flooz and Beenz, as we saw earlier.

These visions seem to be derived more from a middle-class idealist than a revolutionary anti-government would-be drug kingpin or radical libertarian economic thinker.

It, therefore, seems fair to say that Satoshi is leaning libertarian but not a revolutionary in the political or activist sense. Indeed he explicitly rejects such revolutionary leanings. He distrusted the government but was not explicitly anti-government. He seems informed by more middle-class concerns like subscriptions, privacy, reward points, donations, and spouses and reads the paper.

Summary of Satoshi's Profile

Not much can be said with certainty about Satoshi. Still, we do have a few solid clues based on primary sources for the profile in descending order of certainty: He is in all probability male, British, living in Europe/United Kingdom probably in the London area. Probably born in the early 1970s with a long academic education probably in computer science or mathematics. Programs in C++. He is working full-time as an academic, researcher, or consultant in the IT security area. Not a revolutionary but an idealist with libertarian leanings. He may be married and living a stable middle-class family life. When it comes to skills, he has deep knowledge of proof of work, peer-to-peer technologies, virtual currencies, and private key encryption.

CHAPTER 7

The Usual Suspects?

As we saw earlier, the proposed identities of Satoshi seemed to be in need of revision. The profile that we have made further supports the conclusion that the real identity of Satoshi has yet to be found in previous attempts. The most robust piece of forensic evidence we have is that Satoshi is British and based in London. None of the earlier suspects fit that fact. It is necessary to look beyond the usual suspects.

We, therefore, have to find a way to expand the search. The best way to do that is again to look at the primary sources written by Satoshi himself. As we have seen, he does not write explicitly about himself or any collaborators, but the Bitcoin whitepaper references several other researchers. In academic circles, citing teachers, collaborators, and, most of all, oneself is very common. This opens a new and exciting way of approaching the search: could Satoshi have cited himself? Even if he didn't, we would get a good clue as to the social and academic circles in which he is to be found. Let us, therefore, go back to the list of references we can find in the Bitcoin whitepaper.

Redrawing the List of Suspects

The Bitcoin whitepaper features eight references with a total of ten different people. In the Appendix, I present a detailed analysis of who they are and to what extent they fit the profile of Satoshi. The citation list is one of many clues we have about where to find who could be Satoshi. From the whitepaper, we can deduce that he was most inspired by Adam Back's

© Anders Lisdorf 2023
A. Lisdorf, *Still Searching for Satoshi*, https://doi.org/10.1007/978-1-4842-9639-4_7

Hashcash and Wei Dai's B-money. Probably the only place where these ideas were discussed in detail was on the cypherpunk mailing list, where Back and Dai announced them at the end of the 1990s. There is a good chance that the historical Satoshi would have been part of that community and learned about Hashcash and B-money from there. Since the list contained thousands of members interested in cryptography in general, they were not all interested in the relative niche of virtual currencies. We should therefore narrow the scope to those members who actively engaged in discussions around Hashcash and B-money. Satoshi would be likely to have done that.

Hashcash was presented to the list in the spring of 1997. It was discussed on a few occasions after that. B-money was proposed on the mailing list in the fall of 1998. It was also discussed subsequently on a few occasions. All in all, both proposals did not attract a lot of attention, but still, a significant number of people responded. Altogether 19 identifiable persons engaged with Dai and Back to give feedback and ask questions about these two ideas.

This yields a list of 29 people who could, in principle, be the historical Satoshi. In Table 7-1 we can see the degree to which they match the criteria of the profile we constructed. M means that we have evidence that the person matches the criteria. D means we have evidence that the person deviates and does not match the criteria, while U means that it is unknown based on the evidence I have been able to find.

Table 7-1. *Analysis of match between potential historical people and Satoshi*

Name	Male	British Language	Born in the 1970s	Based in Europe/UK	University education	Academic/Consultant	Programs C++	Married	Libertarian leaning	Proof-of-work	Peer-to-peer	Virtual currencies	Private key encryption
Wei Dai	M	D	M	D	M	D	M	U	M	M	D	M	M
Jean-Jacques Quisquater	M	D	D	M	M	M	D	U	U	M	D	D	M
Xavier Serret Avila	M	D	M	M	M	M	M	U	U	D	D	D	M
Henri Massias	M	D	M	M	M	M	M	U	U	D	D	D	M
Stuart Haber	M	D	D	D	M	M	D	U	U	M	D	D	M
Wakefield Scott Stornetta	M	D	D	D	M	M	D	U	M	M	D	D	M
David Allen Bayer	M	D	D	D	M	M	D	U	U	D	D	D	M
Ralph C. Merkle	M	D	D	D	M	M	D	U	U	M	D	D	M
William Feller	M	D	D	D	M	M	D	U	U	D	D	D	D
Adam Back	M	M	M	M	M	M	M	M	M	M	M	M	M
Anil Dash	M	D	U	U	U	U	U	U	U	U	U	U	U
Paul E. Foley	M	D	U	D	U	U	U	U	U	U	U	U	U
Paul Bradley	M	M	U	M	M	M	D	U	U	D	D	D	M
Kent Crispin	M	D	D	D	M	M	M	U	U	D	D	D	D
Steve Schear	M	D	D	D	U	D	U	U	M	U	M	M	M
Robert Costner	M	D	U	D	U	D	U	U	M	U	U	U	U
Joe Randall Farmer	M	D	U	D	U	U	U	U	U	U	U	U	U
Timothy C. May	M	D	D	D	M	D	D	U	M	D	D	M	D
William H. Geiger III	M	D	U	U	U	D	D	U	M	D	D	D	M
Robert Hettinga	M	D	D	D	M	M	D	U	M	D	D	M	D
Michael Johnson	M	D	D	D	M	D	U	M	D	U	U	U	M
Ge' Weijers	M	D	D	D	M	D	U	U	U	U	U	U	U
Andy Dustman	M	D	D	D	M	D	D	U	U	D	M	D	M
Bill Frantz	M	D	D	D	M	U	U	U	U	D	D	M	M
Duncan Frissell	M	D	D	D	M	D	D	U	M	D	D	D	D
Jim Choate	M	D	U	D	U	U	U	U	U	U	M	U	U
Mark Fisher	M	D	U	D	U	D	D	U	U	D	D	D	D
Ian Grigg	M	D	D	D	M	M	U	U	M	M	U	M	M
Dave Birch	M	M	D	M	U	M	D	U	D	U	U	M	U

A glance at the table shows that all are male and probably all are university educated. But apart from that, some people match some aspects, whereas others match different ones. No profile criteria are uniquely matched to anyone.

We can also see that almost all have at least a handful of criteria that do not match the profile and, therefore, cannot have been the historical person behind Satoshi. But we also see that one individual stands out and matches all parts of the profile. That individual is Adam Back. This does not necessarily mean that Adam Back is Satoshi. He is the only one who matches all the essential criteria of the profile and should therefore be looked at in more detail.

A Closer Look at Adam Back

Like most cypherpunks, he is a private person who does not share much about himself, but we can piece together the most essential facts from various sources. He was born in 1970 in London and completed his A levels in mathematics, physics, and economics. His English is decidedly British, and his writing is flawless. He completed his PhD in computer science from the University of Exeter in 1995 on the topic of distributed computing. The code written for the thesis was written in C++. He was a cypherpunk, a very active cryptography mailing list contributor, and particularly interested in virtual currencies.

Regarding identifying Satoshi, it is not the first time Back has been evaluated as Satoshi: Dominic Frisby entertained the notion that he could be Satoshi but discarded it because Back confessed to him that he preferred C to C++. Frisby failed to notice that Back had used C++ extensively as the basis for his PhD and was probably working in that language when Bitcoin was being developed. He also concluded from his first post on Bitcoin Talk that Back was only just learning about Bitcoin. That is an astounding conjecture. Others like the YouTuber Barely

Sociable, who also identified Adam Back as Satoshi, have correctly noted how incredibly deeply into the details he seems to be right from the get-go. He immediately starts contributing detailed ideas for improvements.

Let us look at other evidence to help us evaluate whether Back was Satoshi. Most of it has been supplied by the above-mentioned YouTuber, Barely Sociable, who provided incredible forensic detective work. We will get back to that shortly.

The Absence of Back from Bitcoin

The first thing to notice is Back's absence in all early discussions about Bitcoin in the early days. Not until his introduction to Bitcoin Talk in 2013 did he engage in Bitcoin. This is a man who has been on a quest for a virtual currency like Bitcoin since 1997. Consider a reply in April 1997, where he called for an electronic cash system on the cryptography mailing list:

The cryptographic requirements for a system such as this would be:

1) *anonymous (privacy preserving, payee and payer anonymous*

2) *distributed (to make it hard to shut down)*

3) *have some built in scarcity*

4) *require no trust of any one individual*

5) *preferably offline (difficult to do with pure software)*

6) *reusable*

This is virtually a road map for Bitcoin more than ten years before its release, and Back takes no verifiable interest in Bitcoin for almost five years. People can of course change interests over time, so this does not prove anything by itself. It seems safe to conclude that Back at least had the motive to build Bitcoin.

Back-Satoshi Interactions

Another curious fact is that Satoshi corresponded with all key players in the field of cryptographic virtual currencies, Hal Finney, Wei Dai, and Nick Szabo, except Adam Back. It is alleged that Satoshi communicated with Back, but once we look closer at the evidence, it does not seem strong. We know about this interaction from two late sources. The first is an email made public by Wei Dai in which Satoshi mentions communication with Back. The email is dated August 22, 2008, and Satoshi writes to Dai: "Adam Back (hashcash.org) noticed the similarities and pointed me to your site." The other is a 2020 interview with Cointelegraph where Back mentions email exchanges with Satoshi around the same time as the emails exchanged with Dai. But unlike Dai, he refused to share them, so there is no way to verify this claim. These emails and interviews are all secondary evidence far removed from when Bitcoin was created. There is, therefore, no good evidence that Back ever communicated with Satoshi.

Other Evidence

Other pieces of evidence are consistent with Adam Back being Satoshi. There is the fact that he uses double spacing after a period when he writes, similar to Satoshi. He is, of course, not unique in this respect since this was a writing style taught to people who started writing on typewriters before writing on computers. He matches the British language and is similarly fluent, with very few errors in his writing.

Another thing to consider is that he has the unique combination of skills Satoshi showed. It is not very common to know about distributed computing, cryptography, and virtual currencies. This is a relatively rare combination, particularly knowing about peer-to-peer computing, which was Back's specialty.

The YouTuber Barely Sociable also points out the fact that Adam Back was filing patents until 2005 and then nothing until again in 2011 when Satoshi stepped back from Bitcoin. He also did not write academic papers during this period. He did not participate in mailing lists from 2007 to 2010. The Hashcash website seems to have stopped being updated in 2004 since no media stories are listed after that point. Back started updating the Wikipedia site about Bitcoin in 2012 but did not get involved until 2013. On Twitter, he followed the discussion about WikiLeaks using Bitcoin attentively. In 2013, when he joined the Bitcoin Talk forum, he referred to an obscure bug that was fixed in 2010 that allowed Satoshi to mine a second hoard of coins that could not be traced to him.

If you compare Adam Back's website and the first version of the Bitcoin website, they are similar in their lack of styling. But this is also standard cypherpunk style.

These are all pieces of circumstantial evidence pointing to Back. Each of them can be explained away individually. What is important is that here we have shown that Adam Back is the only person from a list of possible suspects who fits all aspects of the profile we created for Satoshi. He has the skills and motive to be the inventor of Bitcoin. This, of course, does not prove anything beyond a doubt, but "if it walks like a duck and quacks like a duck…"

But Then Again…

Adam Back maintains that he had email exchanges with Satoshi but will not reveal them due to "netiquette." He holds that it is not okay to reveal personal communication without prior consent. Another curious lead he gave on Bitcoin Talk on May 14, 2013, is an anonymous comment made in 1999 on a cypherpunk email thread. He indicates that this reply might have been by Nakamoto. In this reply, the anonymous respondent suggests an ecash system that solves the double spending problem by a public database, which is distributed by combining it with Hashcash and

B-money. The suggestion does indeed sound a lot like an early vision of Bitcoin. The author even writes with double spacing after a period. He seems to like Back and Dai. In a reply from January 9, 1998, he argues that people like Timothy May, Paul Bradley, and others should leave the list: "This will leave fine thinkers with good hearts like Adam Back, Bill Stewart, Wei Dai, and others, people who still believe that cryptography can make a strong contribution to our freedom." He also demonstrates a relatively deep knowledge of cryptography.

Could this be Satoshi, then? In other replies "Anonymous" seems much more confrontational, and he writes in American English. And if he was Satoshi, why would hesay Back directed him to Dai's work in 2008, and why would he write Dai about a reference suggesting a completely wrong year if he already knew about it since 1999? Or was this actually the post that put Back on the right track to create Bitcoin as Satoshi?

Concluding the Search for Satoshi

As with anything in history, it is difficult to know for sure who the person behind Satoshi is. The purpose of this investigation was to interrogate the available evidence and find out if it was possible to identify a possible suspect. We looked first at the evidence to create a profile of what we knew for certain or found highly likely. Then we started looking for potential suspects to match this profile. This was done by looking at the citations in Satoshi's Bitcoin whitepaper since academics tend to cite research by themselves. Then we looked at evidence of people who had engaged in dialogue about the two ideas that form the basis of the Bitcoin whitepaper: Hashcash and B-money. This was done by combing through the cypherpunk mailing list for all threads about them and listing all the people who responded to these threads. This yielded a list of 29 people that were researched to determine the degree to which they matched the profile criteria. No one matched more than 8 out of 13 criteria except Adam Back. Reviewing additional evidence supported the view that he had the motive, opportunity, and means to create Bitcoin. Back denies this, as we saw anyone being identified as Satoshi would have good reason to. It is, of course, possible that someone else who left no other discernible trace of his interest in this highly specialized niche is Satoshi. It might be the FBI, the Bilderberg group, or just some other "anonymous" genius listening in on conversations and reading research papers. But this is not the simplest explanation. Scientific and historical knowledge proceeds by following the evidence and accepting the simplest explanation, but I will leave it up to the reader to decide who or what created Bitcoin. I only hope to have provided clarity on what our quite substantial evidence actually tells us.

CHAPTER 8

Money

That bitcoin is money may seem straightforward, almost self-evident. You can exchange it for currency, check your account to see your balance, and buy goods and services. But from there, it gets murky since it does not resemble the regular currency we use to pay taxes and buy groceries. What people have come to understand as "normal" money is so-called fiat currencies such as dollars, yen, and euros. The word *fiat* comes from Latin and means "may it be done" or "let it be done." This was the word used in the Vulgate, which was the Latin translation of the Bible, more precisely at the start of the book of Genesis where God uttered, "Let there be light" ("Fiat lux" Genesis 1:3). Modern currencies similarly work by decree, though not entirely sanctioned by God but rather by nation-states, that the money they print has value. One can think of fiat currency in much the same way: "Let it be valuable."

Bitcoin does not work in the same way. There is no divine governmental or another entity sanctioning its value. So to understand bitcoin's meaning, we need to ask, "How does money become money? Or what is money?" and where does Bitcoin fit into that?

The Variety of Money

Before diving into the question of bitcoin as money, let us look at what money is from a broader perspective than modern fiat currencies, a relatively recent and exceptional phenomenon. First, let us consider some examples that show the diversity of money.

© Anders Lisdorf 2023
A. Lisdorf, *Still Searching for Satoshi*, https://doi.org/10.1007/978-1-4842-9639-4_8

The Rossel Islanders

In the tropical sun lies a small isolated island in the easternmost part of the Louisiade Archipelago in Papua New Guinea. It is called Rossel Island. It has a population of only a few thousand. Their language is not related to any other known language and is notoriously difficult to translate. The inhabitants live almost entirely secluded, with little interaction with the outside world. The basic social units on Rossel Island are families living in a few small villages. The economy is centered around subsistence farming with some growing of cash crops. Anthropologist John Liep who worked there for four decades beginning in the 1970s distinguishes three economic spheres: the domestic, commodity, and ceremonial exchange domains.

Exchange in the domestic domain is rendered as kinship services and thus does not necessitate a balance of reciprocity mediated by gifts, barter, or money. This is similar to most cultures where family units help each other without keeping tabs. For example, the most common exchange is help in gardening, which would be paid for by a meal.

The commodity domain involves clothes, kerosene, batteries, and such. This was mediated through cash, which the Rossel islanders earned through labor at plantations or through sales of cash crops. The commodity domain was dominated by Western currency but only related to commodities traded with the outside world. Thus, money was restricted and could only be used to acquire imported commodities.

The ceremonial exchange domain is the main domain for social life on the island, where payments are made for dowries, concerning death and funerals, as well as the central ceremony of the pig feast. In this domain, payments are made with the local type of shell money called ndap and ke. They derive from two different species of seashell and have different values.

The ndap is the most valuable and is further subdivided into three groups. The very high division is rare; probably less than a hundred shells exist. The high division is only slightly more prevalent, while substantially more shells exist from the low division. Liep estimates that only 20,000 shells exist in total, averaging 41 per household.

Exchanges, as part of bridewealth, follow complex patterns where a specific number from the different divisions needs to be produced over several payments. Similarly, at the pig feast, different parts of the pig can be purchased for different types of ndap. The very high division was previously only used for the most important exchanges, like the taking of human life as compensation to the relatives of the murdered victim. They are no longer used as payments but can be used as securities against loans.

The high division plays an important role in the ceremonial exchange system. One of the shells from this category is usually given as the first payment in a bridewealth sealing the marriage contract. It can also be used for the main part of the pig at a pig feast or for houses or canoes. The low division circulates more freely, but not like Western money. These are often used for payment in higher numbers for parts of the pig at the pig feast and all other exchanges.

The ke is a string of ten shells common across the Pacific Ocean, and even fewer exist. Liep estimates only 2,500 in total. They are less valuable than the ndap and form their own ranked classification system denoting the value. A conversion rate between ke and the low division of ndap establishes a cross between these two currencies.

The shell money of Rossel Island is thus used for goods and services that are traditional for the inhabitants, like marriage, funerals, feasts, and the building of canoes and houses. Western money can't be used in this sphere. Western money is used for commodities acquired from the outside world and only there. In the domestic sphere, kinship forms a framework for exchanging services such as help with gardening and other domestic types of work.

Cigarettes

"Black market activities are playing havoc with the economy in most countries in Europe and cigarettes are supplanting national currencies as legal tender. 12 dozen fresh eggs for 100 cigarettes. Swedish silk stockings for 35 cigarettes a pair," a returned Canadian airman was quoted saying in the *Saskatchewan* newspaper in January 1946. In the aftermath of World War II, black markets emerged due to food shortages and a general economic downturn. Cigarettes were used as an alternative form of payment in these markets. It was not because national fiat currencies had disappeared but because inflation was high. In Germany, foreign currency exchange was restricted, which led to cigarettes taking over as a medium of exchange. It was also used by people who did not smoke and thus acquired value surpassing their commodity value.

This is not a unique event arising out of special circumstances. The same happened in the Yugoslavian civil war at the beginning of the 1990s and was even documented in the recent war in Ukraine under the Russian occupation of Kherson. Cigarettes seem to continuously pop up as currency in connection with war.

But cigarettes also seem to take on the role of money in other contexts. In American and British prisons, where inmates do not have access to money, they have long held the role of alternative currency for goods and services traded among the inmates, even if they have recently been eclipsed by ramen noodles, which are also healthier.

It can be seen that under certain circumstances, a commodity like cigarettes can take on the role of money. This seems to happen when the smooth function of the monetary system is somehow impeded: in prisons, currency is plainly unavailable in post-war Europe. It was either consciously limited by blocking foreign currency exchange or inconvenient due to high inflation. In modern wars, using cigarettes instead of money happened when exchange with the outside world was constrained. Alternative currencies can thus emerge at different times under different circumstances.

Points

Around 2009, the Danish retailer Coop relaunched their loyalty program called Coop Plus. Here members could get rewarded in points rather than the local Danish currency, crowns (I was myself involved in the implementation of this). The points were pegged to crowns at a fixed rate. When you shopped in Coop's stores, you received points. These could be redeemed in an online store where points could be used alongside crowns to pay for products.

Once a year, any balance of points would be released for store purchases. The exchange rate would be used to convert to crowns. The customer could access their virtual wallet with these funds by scanning the membership card. It was impossible to withdraw or purchase points. Only purchases would generate these points. Coop thus seemingly minted currency for their members. From an accounting perspective, this was not what happened. Rather the points were considered a deferred discount. The points were thus considered a right to a future discount.

It is common in retail to offer rewards. Today, almost any modern retailer has some sort of loyalty program where members can get rewards. Often these are discounts or rewards, but points are still used in some places. It is commonly restricted to the same company's stores, but more generic reward programs have been known.

The Many Facets of Money

These examples give us just a small taste of the versatility and plurality of money. We can see that even a small society like the Rossel islanders can employ many types of money, serving different economic spheres. They can also be used as loan collaterals, and exchange rates exist between different currencies. The example of cigarettes emerging as alternative money shows us that different types of money can emerge and disappear depending on the circumstances of a society. In contrast, the existence of loyalty scheme points shows that alternative money can happily exist alongside common currency in normal times too.

What Is Money?

The preceding examples show that it is not clear where the line between money and not money is. There are many definitions of money. In his monumental work, *A History of Money*, Glyn Davies defines money as "(...) that which is universally recognized by the consumer and user as holding value as a commodity that can be exchanged for goods within the economy, and it does not have to have any characteristic, state-mandated or other, in order to function" (Davies, p. xxix). This is a good starting point to clarify what we mean by money. Others have defined it differently, but for this investigation, I think this definition points to some key points about money:

> It is a commodity.

> It is universally seen as holding value.

> It can be exchanged for goods and services.

Being a commodity means that one instance of a unit of money is the same as another. This is unlike artwork, for example, where a more detailed assessment of each piece has to be done to assess its value. Money also needs people to agree that it has value. It is not enough that one individual believes it has value. On the other hand, all it takes for money is for people to believe it has value. There is no inherent quality in anything that can be used to define it as money. The last part relates to how money can be used. It is not enough that something is universally considered valuable, like time or fair weather; it needs to be used for exchange.

Functions of Money

In *Money and the Mechanism of Exchange* from 1875, the English economist William Stanley Jevons distinguished four functions of money: a medium of exchange, a common measure of value, a standard of value (or standard of deferred payment), and a store of value.

Building on his insights, it is common in modern economics to distinguish three key functions of money: a medium of exchange, a unit of account, and a store of value subsuming the standard of value function in the others. Money must fulfill at least these three functions to work as money. Glyn Davies mentions ten different functions, so this is not an exact science. For the sake of simplicity, let us look at the consensus of most modern treatments of money and look into the three key functions of money.

Medium of Exchange

A medium of exchange is any object generally accepted for exchanging goods and services. We saw previously how commodities like seashells, cigarettes, and points can become a medium of exchange. This medium should be possible to use across several different goods and services to fulfill this function but not necessarily all. Consider the example of casino chips or tokens at an arcade or laundromat. They are used as a medium of exchange, but the range of the economic sphere they apply is too limited to say they fulfill the function of money. Loyalty points apply to the whole range of goods a retailer offers but only to that particular retailer. A medium of exchange can thus be limited to a particular sphere, as we also saw with Western money on Rossel Island being restricted as a medium of exchange only for imported goods.

Throughout history, different objects have been used as mediums of exchange. In particular, commodities have been used for this. Across the globe, cattle have served and still serve as a powerful medium of exchange. This has also been the case historically in Europe and the Western world, as evidenced in the English vocabulary. The term *pecuniary*, meaning "relating to or consisting of money," derives from the Latin *pecuniarius*, which comes from the Latin *pecus* (cattle). Cattle have historically been used as a medium of exchange, particularly for larger things like bridewealth. Although big, it is a somewhat convenient medium of exchange since it can move by itself and inconvenient since it is not easily divisible.

Luckily other commodities can serve this function better for smaller goods and services. Salt is another example of a universal and convenient medium of exchange that has also made it into our language. The English word *salary* similarly derives from the Latin word *salarium*, which comes from the word *sal*, meaning "salt." In Roman times salt was a scarce and valuable commodity. In contrast to cattle, it was easy to subdivide and hence better suited as a medium of exchange for goods and services of lower value.

Unit of Account

A unit of account is a standard numerical measurement of the value of goods or services. We saw how cigarettes became a unit of account for the payment of eggs or stockings. Similarly, the ndap shells on Rossel Island specify how much is to be paid for a bride. It can thus be used to compare the relative value of two different goods or goods and services. A unit of account is also necessary for deferred payments, as we saw in the example of points that were deferred discounts. It does not mean that payments are made in this unit. It can be made in other units or goods that make up a specific quantity.

Such could happen if, for example, you go to a flea market and find a nice oak table. After haggling appropriately, you agree with the seller that it is worth 100 dollars. Unfortunately, you do not have that in cash. But you just bought a vintage lamp at another stand that the seller is interested in. You agree that it is worth 40 dollars. You also have 50 Canadian dollars from your trip to Vancouver last week. The value converted to dollars is about 35. Luckily your wife has the remaining 25 dollars in cash that she lets you borrow until you get home.

Notice that you provided no money in the unit of account for this exchange. The unit of account is American dollars, but the lamp is a good, the Canadian dollars are another currency, and the remaining portion was provided through debt. Neither of these would be sufficient individually to purchase the oak table, but because of a common unit of account, it was possible to facilitate an exchange anyway.

Basically, anything could be used as a unit of account as long as it is measurable. We can imagine length, heat, voltage, or pressure being used as a unit of account, but this is difficult to measure in practice. Historically two types of measurement have dominated: count and weight. Of these, the count is more versatile. This was used for cowry shells, beaver skins, and the like. This works well when the unit is fungible or very similar in quality. This does not work well for diamonds, for example. Although they are universally viewed as valuable, they must be individually assessed.

Weight has been even more dominating, at least in Western Europe. The British pound derives from the value of a pound of sterling silver. Only later was this converted into coins representing a (now abstract) pound. The Latin "libra," which is the source of the French livre, is similarly a unit of weight. The challenge with weight and why it did not last as the preferred unit of account is that one needs scales to measure it. This is more prone to fraud since the scales can be tampered with. Also, the substance can be tampered with. If a precious metal like silver is used for payment, it can be mixed with a non-precious metal like tin.

Store of Value

The last of the major functions of money is as a store of value, which is perhaps the most critical and controversial. Ideally, money should function as a store of value, so it is possible to defer consumption into the future. Some economists argue that money's function as a store of value is the most important.

The concept is straightforward. If one earns $100 and decides to save it for a year, the money should also be worth $100 in a year's time. This is, unfortunately, rarely the case. Frequently the $100 will be worth a fraction like, say, $90. That is due to inflation. Inflation undermines money's function as a store of value. This is unfortunate if you had your mind set on a particularly nice pair of pants. On the other hand, if you borrowed $1,000, you would now only have to repay $900 and have thus earned $100.

The opposite can also happen, where the $100 would be worth, say, $110. This is more attractive if you want to save and defer consumption, but not if you have debt. If you borrowed $1,000, you would now have to pay back $1,100.

As can be seen, money's function as a store of value has important implications for the economy. Very high inflation, that is, when money is particularly bad as a store of value, is crippling for an economy. This is also when alternative currencies or commodities, like cigarettes or gold, prop up. But another thing to make a mental note of, since it will be important later, is that the store of value function is tied closely to debt.

If you have a lot of debt denoted in a currency, you would be rooting for it as a bad store of value. On the other hand, if you are a creditor or saver, you would want it to be as good a store of value as possible. Historically commodities like precious metals have served and still serve as significant stores of value without being used as money. This has to do with the problem of their unit of measure being weight.

There is no precise formula for determining what makes something a good store of value. We will return to this topic, but for now, we can highlight that the most important quality is durability. Any commodity that vanishes quickly will logically be a poor store of value. This is probably also why gold and precious metals in many cultures have been used as stores of value. Gold doesn't tarnish even after millions of years. Iron corrodes comparatively fast, and so does copper. Cowries and other seashells have the same quality; they do not vanish, which may also account for their enduring success worldwide.

History of Money and Exchange

The experience of the modern world where we walk to the grocery store to shop for dinner or to the cafe for an oat milk cinnamon latte or pay the rent online may take as self-evident the existence of money. It feels almost as integrated a part of human existence as clothes and music. That is, however, far from the case historically. We already saw the diversity of money, but let us trace how humanity ended up in the current situation where money dominates our lives.

Exchange

First, we need to step back to the basic problem that money solves, and that is exchange. The ability to exchange food, goods, and other services with other fellow members of the species that are not direct descendants is not uniquely human. Ants do this systematically, as do bees. Primates also have some idea of exchange, but this ability took center stage when humans diverged evolutionarily from primates. As cognitive scientist Michael Tomasello has argued, humans are unique in their ability to hunt together and share the spoils. In *A Natural History of Human Thinking*, he suggests that *Homo heidelbergensis* was the first human species to engage in collaborative hunts two million years ago. The nature of a collaborative hunt necessitates exchange. Each participant in the hunt receives a piece of the prey in exchange for their participation in the hunt. This is evidenced by the prey that *Homo heidelbergensis* killed, such as large game animals. They would only have been able to kill it with their tools if they collaborated in a group.

That the capacity for exchange became a mainstay of human civilization is evidenced by one of the grandfathers of modern anthropology Marcel Mauss in his classic essay "The Gift: The Form and Reason for Exchange in Archaic Societies" from 1950. In this work, he investigated how the exchange of objects builds cohesion in human

119

groups. He argued that exchange was not a new concept but extended deep into prehistory, which he showed through an impressive array of evidence from societies around the globe, contemporary and historical. The most basic form of exchange is the gift. This is a common way objects move between individuals and groups in all societies.

Gift exchange can form the basis of a gift economy, as first evidenced by another legend in anthropology and a contemporary of Mauss, Bronislaw Malinowski, who documented how the gift formed the basis of an economy around the same time on the Trobriand Islands. The gift works through reciprocity, the expectation of a return. Mauss was the first to argue that the act of giving in itself carried the promise of return. A gift is never free in human societies.

Barter

According to most treatments of the history of money, the first stage is barter, which can be seen as a more focused and immediate form of exchange building on reciprocity like the gift economy. The difference is that gift-giving is less specified regarding the nature and timing of reciprocity. In barter, the precise nature and timing of the exchange are put into effect.

Unfortunately, barter suffers from several structural problems. The first is the lack of a common standard of value. If someone wants to exchange apricots for knives, it is not straightforward how the apricots should be valued vis-a-vis the knives. You might work out that one knife is 120 apricots, which would make barter straightforward for this particular case, but these are just two products; what about tea or farmwork or milk? Each product pairing needs some exchange ratio to work smoothly and be predictable. This quickly becomes infeasible as the number of goods and services traded on the market increases.

The next challenge is sometimes called the problem of double coincidence of wants. If I own an orchard and have excess apricots that I want to give away and I need a knife, then I need to find someone with excess knives who wants apricots. The double coincidence is necessary for the exchange to take place. That is perhaps not impossible, but unlikely, particularly in smaller societies.

The last problem is how to store value. Come harvest, I might have an abundance of apricots from my orchard that I can use to barter for things I need, but they will spoil quickly. Outside the harvest season, I will have nothing of value to trade, which is inconvenient. This is the case for all perishable goods, which are mostly food. Knives are durable and thus better for barter.

These facts about barter restrict the utility of barter as the backbone of an economic system. This is why an improvement of the barter system often develops where a few preferred barter items are used. Examples of such preferred barter items are cattle and salt, which we have already seen, but also wheat, rice, sugar, and blankets are commonly used as preferred barter items. These items can then be used as references for other goods. Perhaps 100 apricots are worth one blanket, and a knife is five blankets. Then I will know what to expect to pay. With a few preferred barter items, remembering market prices is manageable, which minimizes the problems of double coincidence of wants and standard of value. I can now go to the market with my cart of apricots and exchange them for blankets and then find someone to exchange a knife for them. This will work even if the knife trader does not want my apricots, and it also solves my store of value problem since the spare blankets can be stored through the winter.

Primitive Money

Preferred barter is only a small step away from what is sometimes called primitive money. There are different ideas about what precisely primitive money is. In *The Origins of Money*, Philip Grierson considers it to be

"all money that is not coin like or modern paper money a derivative
of the coin." This tells us to look for things based on our modern
conceptualization of money as coin or paper but defers the question of
what money actually is. A more operational conceptualization is offered by
Paul Einzig in his book *Primitive Money in Its Ethnological, Historical, and
Economic Aspects* from 1966: "a unit or object conforming to a reasonable
degree to some standard of uniformity, which is employed for reckoning or
for making a large portion of the payments in the community concerned."
This quotation points to some key attributes, such as the objects'
uniformity and that they function as a unit of account and medium of
exchange in a larger community. Now we start to see something that starts
to fulfill the three functions of money. Many different kinds of objects have
served as primitive money.

Historically commodities have been widely used. We have already seen
how cattle and salt were employed, but grain was even more important.
The Mesopotamian culture was the first to develop accounting, and this
was to keep track of the amount of grain deposited to and withdrawn from
warehouses. In Egypt, grain was the basis of the economy over thousands
of years and facilitated the building of monumental architectural works
like the pyramids. These commodities were used because they were
ubiquitous and stable in peoples' lives.

These commodities all have utility in themselves. Cows, salt, and
grain can be eaten. Other types of primitive money do not share this
characteristic. The ubiquitous cowries, for example, have no immediate
use and are completely symbolic. People used them from prehistoric times
around the Pacific and Indian Oceans. It comes from the shell of a mollusk
that lives here, particularly around the Maldive Islands. Even in ancient
China, the cowrie was used, so much so that the pictogram for money in
Chinese is a cowrie.

Metals were used from the late Stone Age and became central for toolmaking and weapons. This helped facilitate their use as money. For example, the Chinese made metal cowrie replicas in the late Stone Age. Tools and weapons were also known to be used as money. Caesar, for example, related how the Britons he encountered used swords as currency. Metal has been used in different shapes and forms, such as rods and coils or even just uneven lumps.

Banking

The next big transition in the history of money was banking. A specialized bureaucracy developed alongside when money became representational, as it did in ancient Mesopotamia in writing on cuneiform tablets. This facilitated the development of banking. Indeed, as the anthropologist and Occupy Wall Street organizer David Graeber argues in his book *Debt: The First 5000 Years*, debt is so entangled with money as to be indistinguishable. They appear at the same time, and Graeber contends "a history of debt (...) is thus necessarily a history of money." This view has much to offer since the ability to use debt is greatly amplified by money. Writing can even be said to have developed from the need to keep track of debt. The earliest texts from the city of Uruk from around 3,100 BCE are livestock lists.

In this context, in the ancient Near East, banking developed. The oldest Babylonian private banking firms were anonymous, but we know of one called the "Grandsons of Egibi," with headquarters in Babylon. They offered a suite of banking services. They gave out loans against various securities and offered deposits from which customers could withdraw the whole or parts with checks. Babylonian banks also financed infrastructure building, such as irrigation canals, and offered leasing arrangements.

But it was in Egypt that the so-called giro-banking system was perfected. In Egypt, grain had become the major type of currency, and state warehouses functioned effectively as banks, where grain could be deposited and withdrawn at will. Here a system was developed whereby an owner of a deposit could transfer part of his deposit to the king as tax through a written order. This system became generalized as a way to settle debts for the people of Egypt, and thus the first known instance of giro-banking came into existence.

Most banking functions have been documented in the ancient Near East as early as the third millennium BCE. Curiously, these preceded the use of coins and metal as money by more than a thousand years, whereas in the West, it was the other way around where coins preceded the first banks by more than a thousand years. Consequently, we can see no unidirectional relation between coins and banking functions. Let us then jump to the history of coins.

Coins

The modern conception of money is intimately related to coins, that is, a piece of metal minted and authorized by someone. The invention of coins can be traced to China. Here metal representations of cowrie shells had been in use before. Chinese coins were made of base metals that were not worth a lot and consequently only used for smaller purchases. Interestingly the word *cash* derives from this type of Chinese money brought to Europe by the Portuguese, who opened a sea route to China. The Tamil word for these was *cash*.

In Europe, coins took a different path because they were minted on precious metals like gold and silver. The Western invention of coins happened in Lydian and Ionian Greece in Asia Minor. There are many contributing factors to why it happened then and there, but the key among these was that this area had rivers with rich deposits of gold and silver. Around this time, the cities of Lydia and Ionia were among the wealthiest and sitting on the rim of the great Near Eastern empires with whom they traded. Coins emerged initially from crude versions in the middle of the sixth century BCE to become standardized and beautiful pieces of artwork in the fifth century.

From this time, the world did not look back. The coin became the dominant form of money since it performs the three functions of money well. It is easily used as a medium of exchange. Especially precious metal money can be used for high-value purchases as well as low value since the weight and volume are manageable. The standardization of money and the minting paradigm where an authority signs the coins facilitate standardization and make coins easy to use as units of account. Since precious metals were used, coins were also convenient as stores of value. Precious metals have the convenient feature that they are scarce and widely dispersed. As long as no sudden increase in their extraction was made, the value would remain stable, which it did.

The Invention of Money

As we saw, the basic function of money is to facilitate exchange. Historically this has been done through other methods like gift-giving and barter. Through the path of preferred barter, the idea of primitive money won. They were often based on commodities with some utility, but purely symbolic or representational objects like seashells and metals became common. These primitive forms of money became the basis of purely representational money used in banking services. In ancient Egypt, they had a ledger documenting who owned what and allowing transactions between accounts without any physical exchange.

Eventually, this led to the invention of precious metal coins that were ideally suited for commerce. It is important to emphasize that there is no unidirectional path between these different types of exchange nor are they mutually exclusive. Barter can be and is used alongside currency systems. It is also dynamic since societies can revert to barter or primitive money when the monetary system collapses. While there are different stages in the history of money, it seems more appropriate to talk about phases and focus on how individual examples of money fulfill the basic functions of money in concrete historical contexts. Let us, therefore, look closer at the dynamics of money.

Dynamics of Money

Money is a fickle object that is difficult to pin down. It seems to be always in motion. Different mediums are used as money, and the value goes up and down. Periods of stability are the exception rather than the norm from a historical perspective. That does not mean that every money-related event is completely novel and incomprehensible. It is possible to distinguish certain key factors that influence the dynamics of money.

Key Factors of Money

Four key factors are important to understand the dynamics of money. They are the standard for money, minting, legal tender, and supply and demand.

Standard

While money can be based on commodities like grain, which has some utility, it can also be completely symbolic, like modern currencies or cowrie shells that have no utility outside their function as money. The most successful type of money was the precious metal coin. In ancient Greece and Rome times, it was primarily silver that was used as the medium for making coins (while the Persians preferred gold). Silver was thus the standard for this type of money. Designs could change, but the ultimate value was derived from silver itself. This is called a silver standard. The standard is what the value of money is pegged against, that is, where the money ultimately derives its value from. If the price of this peg changes, like it did when silver mining suddenly produced significantly more silver, the value of money on the silver standard will be affected.

Recently the gold standard has been more successful. The gold standard was a worldwide standard from the 1870s until the 1920s and again from after World War II until 1971. Under the gold standard, currencies were pegged to the value of gold, which made it easy and transparent what the value of money was. All currencies could be calculated against and exchanged for gold. It is not only physical commodities that can serve as a standard. After the collapse of the gold standard, the American dollar took its place as a standard for international trade. Other currencies can similarly serve as this standard reserve currency that can serve as a safe store of value.

When a standard has been in place internationally, like the gold, silver, or dollar standard, this has brought stability to international trade because prices would not fluctuate significantly. The consequence is that investing or storing wealth becomes easier since the price of goods is more predictable.

Minting

A key concern for any type of money is who is allowed to mint it. A money system where anyone can make their own money quickly implodes. Historically mints had a seal or another mechanism to prove that the coin was authorized and correct. The seal proved to people that it was indeed a real coin. The invention of the serrated edges ensured it was also not cut. Several techniques of the mint improved the utility of the coin.

After the success of nation-states as the primary mode of social organization, the authority to mint money was guarded closely by the governments of these nations. They imposed a monopoly on minting money. Curiously, this was not the case in the United States until late in its history. Until the eighteenth century, local currencies thrived in the United States. Local banks issued them, and one had to exchange the local currency when traveling. With a single currency came the convenience of having a shared medium of exchange and the necessity to monopolize the minting of money. Since the monetary system underpins the economy, laws regulating money minting and enforcement tend to be severe.

This is something many inventive virtual currency enthusiasts have felt. We saw how the Liberty dollar and other similar schemes that could be considered alternative currencies were targeted. Indeed this particular dynamic might very well be why Satoshi chose to write under a pseudonym.

Cryptocurrency enthusiasts have not been slow to observe that with this privilege comes great responsibility, which they feel modern states have not handled well since they indiscriminately print money leading to inflation. But this is another problem due to nation-states' controlling the minting of fiat currencies. A lack of control with minting altogether will lead to a general distrust in money and devaluing the currency.

Legal Tender

Perhaps the most important factor is the one defined by legal tender. Legal tender is the form of money that courts of law are obliged to recognize as payment. Each jurisdiction defines its legal tender. In most modern states, it is fiat currency. Legal tender specifies not just the currency but also the particular types of banknotes and coins to be recognized for payment. Sometimes a particular banknote or coin is withdrawn from circulation, which renders it worthless. It also happens that the entire currency, which is accepted as legal tender, switches. This has happened frequently in recent times in Europe, where countries have adopted the new euro currency. In Germany, for example, the Deutch Mark stopped being legal tender, and the euro became the new currency.

The question of legal tender is tied to the question of jurisdiction. Since nation-states in our time are sovereign, the governments of those states define what is legal tender. As of the time of writing, bitcoin has been accepted as legal tender only in El Salvador and the Central African Republic. These are small countries, and it is doubtful what effect it has had on Bitcoin. Still, if larger jurisdictions like the EU or United States were to accept Bitcoin as legal tender, this would significantly improve the utility of Bitcoin.

Supply and Demand

In the sixteenth century, the Spanish theologian Martin de Azpilcueta observed that the prices of commodities changed based on their scarcity. He was the first to develop the law of supply and demand. This states that a traded item on a free market will settle at a price where the quantity demanded will equal the quantity supplied. The consequence is that if either demand or supply is changed, this will affect the price of the commodity. The price increases if demand increases and supply is stable. Conversely, the price will fall if supply increases and demand remains the same.

This observation of the dynamic of prices forms one of the fundamental laws of modern economics. It is interesting in itself, but what Azpilcueta realized was that money itself was also subject to the law of supply and demand. Money itself is a commodity. If the money supply is increased and demand remains the same, the value of money will decrease. This is why the silver and gold standards, in particular, have been successful historically. Precious metals, as opposed to base metals, have a natural scarcity that curtails their supply. Money can only be supplied according to the amount of mined precious metals.

Saifedean Ammous explains how this dynamic works relative to the metals that have served as standards for money. It may come as no surprise that of the precious metals, gold is the most scarce metal in the earth's crust. Silver is also scarce but less so.

Bronze is even more common but still scarce. This corresponds to the relative value of these metals, which is also seen in their use at competitions such as the Olympics, where gold, silver, and bronze medals are given for first, second, and third places. Ammous points out that the real reason behind this is the stock-to-flow ratio, the amount produced relative to the global stock. He shows that for gold, the amount of gold extraction has been surprisingly constant, around 2% of the stock for at least a hundred years. Silver is around 10–15%. That means the stock-to-flow ratio is about 60 for gold since it takes 60 years of production to match the current stock. For silver, it is 5, while for copper, it is less than 1.

The stock-to-flow ratio, in turn, explains why gold fared so well as a standard of money and silver less so. When the amount of silver being extracted increased, the value fell. It also explains why the Chinese use of iron ensured that their coins never acquired more value than was sufficient for smaller purchases.

How Money Becomes Valuable

We are now closer to a point where we can understand the dynamics of money and how money's value changes with other factors. This is illustrated in Figure 8-1.

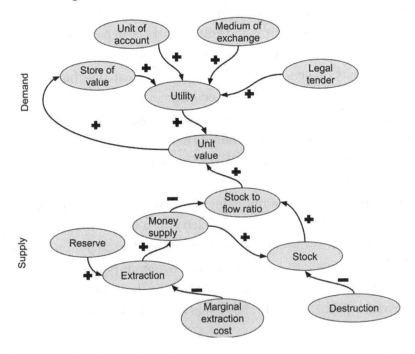

Figure 8-1. *The dynamics of money*

First, a note about how the figure is read. The arrow indicates the direction of influence. A plus means that the source and target move together in the same direction, that is, when the source goes up, the target goes up. Conversely, when the source goes down, the target goes down. The minus indicates an inverse relationship between the source and the target. If the source goes down, the target goes up and vice versa. Of particular interest are loops. A loop with pluses all the way around is a reinforcing loop, while one with pluses and minuses is a balancing loop.

The figure should not be taken to be comprehensive as many other economic factors like velocity, time value, interest rate, the credibility of the issuer, and others also have a significant effect on the dynamics of money. Rather it is meant to highlight a few key factors that have historically been important and continue to be so.

The center of the figure is also the center of interest for any kind of money: the value of a unit of money. An unfavorable change in the value of money could be due to inflation or devaluation. At the same time, a positive change could be due to deflation. It is clear that if a unit has a high or increasing value, it is a good store of value, which creates a reinforcing loop. This is the dynamic behind all asset bubbles. We might best recognize this from the real estate market. When house prices rise, they are seen as a good investment or store of value, and more people buy real estate, increasing the demand and price. This can be seen as a reinforcing loop until the bubble pops. Then the value of real estate drops, and it is no longer a good store of value, which makes the price drop even further. The basic utility of real estate, that is, that it affords shelter, provides a floor below which it will not drop.

The top half of the figure captures the demand-side factors of money, and the bottom half captures the supply side. The demand for money derives from its utility. Remember that the transition from barter to preferred barter to primitive money went through commodities that had a utility due to their potential for consumption, like cattle, salt, and grain. These were then enhanced with the three vital monetary functions when they started being used as money. This positively affected the utility until money proper appeared, where all utility was derived from the monetary functions and not the utility of the base commodity.

Some examples, like gold, may be excellent as a store of value but impractical as a unit of account and especially as a medium of exchange. Minting it into coins increased these functions. Now as coins, they were countable, easily divisible, and small enough to be practical for purchases. The example of Chinese iron coins shows a contrasting case. They were also helpful as per the three functions, but because iron is not equally valuable, larger loads had to be used to make more significant purchases. Consequently, Chinese coins remained niche and were only used for smaller transactions.

This brings us to the lower half, the supply side. We saw how critical the stock-to-flow ratio was for explaining the value of precious metals. Recall that the flow is the amount produced in a year and the stock is the total existing stock. If the money supply is high relative to the stock, the stock-to-flow ratio is low. If the money supply goes up as it did with silver due to increased extraction, the stock-to-flow ratio goes down, which affects the value of the unit. We saw that base metals had a low stock-to-flow ratio, which would account for why the Chinese iron coins were less valuable than the Greek gold and silver coins.

While money supply increases the stock, this should theoretically increase the stock-to-flow ratio, but in practice, the effect of the supply rate is more powerful. Similarly, the destruction of money lowers the stock, which should reduce the stock-to-flow ratio and, thereby, value. We don't see this historically since the destruction of money is always minor compared with the total stock and production of new money.

At the bottom, we see why gold is more valuable than other metals: the reserves in the earth's crust are smaller than other metals. Extraction will increase if extraction costs fall, such as when new mines are discovered or technological advances are made. As we shall see, this is a crucial dynamic that Bitcoin seeks to exploit. Extraction is only relevant when the money supply is based either directly due to minting or indirectly due to being pegged to an extracted commodity like metals. Cowrie shells and beads followed the same dynamic. When markets where they were used were flooded due to improved extraction and production, value plummeted.

Key Dynamics of Money

We are now in a position to see some key dynamics of money that have been observed historically.

The first is the money dynamic. This is when a commodity takes on the function of money by fulfilling one or more of the functions of money. This is what happened to grain in Mesopotamia and cigarettes in post-war Europe. Key to this is the increase in utility of the medium serving as money.

The second is the bubble dynamic. When an asset rises in value, all else being equal, it is a better store of value, which adds to its utility. If this is the main source of the asset's utility, it reinforces the value increase and can create a bubble. Conversely, when it suddenly stops increasing, it quickly falls in value because it is no longer a good store of value.

The third is the supply dynamic. When the supply of money is increased relative to the stock, all else being equal, it lowers the value of the money. This happens during hyperinflation when governments print a lot of money, but also when suddenly new reserves are found of a metal or commodity that serves as the standard of the money.

The fourth is the extraction dynamic. When a commodity depends on extraction, this dynamic is seen. The reserves provide a limit for extraction, and the cost of extraction determines when it is profitable and when the price of the commodity is stable. New deposits or new cheaper extraction techniques thus affect the extraction dynamic.

Bitcoin and Money

Now let us look at Bitcoin. How can these dynamics throw light on bitcoin? Let us try to see if we can use these insights to understand the historical dynamics of bitcoin and the potential future.

Bitcoin as Money

On May 22, 2010, Laszlo Hanyecz purchased pizza with Bitcoin. This was the first documented time Bitcoin took on the function of a medium of exchange. This is a crucial function of money that allows it to be used to procure goods and services. Around the same time, different exchanges popped up that allowed people to exchange Bitcoin for money. As Bitcoin became more well-known, it started to function as a store of value when people exchanged dollars for bitcoin. It can function as a unit of account but has not done so widely in the mainstream economy. It is mostly in black markets and ransomware attacks that bitcoin is the preferred unit of account.

While there has been an increase in vendors that accept bitcoin, such as the occasional hairdresser or cafe, it is far from dramatic. If the average person today came about some bitcoin to burn, they would be hard-pressed to find places to purchase anything. A simple online search for where to buy products with bitcoin reveals that the top list of places where you can actually use bitcoin as a medium of exchange includes Overstock, Newegg, Shopify, Microsoft, Twitch, ProtonMail, NordVPN, Dish Network, and CheapAir. These are, with the exception of Microsoft, not exactly household names. With the possible exception of Shopify, they are all services or software. After being a putative virtual currency for more than ten years, Bitcoin does not impress on this parameter.

As a unit of account, the present state is not much better. Few places use bitcoin as a unit of account and list prices in bitcoin. While I have seen the occasional picture of a sign listing the price in bitcoin, this is always in addition to another currency. In El Salvador, bitcoin is legal tender, but even here, it is not a unit of account. This could change, but there is one structural reason complicating this. Bitcoin is too volatile to be a good unit of account. If vendors need to continuously, even on a daily basis, adjust all of their prices to keep up with the fluctuations, it is not a convenient unit of account.

The third function as a store of value has, above all, been the major success of bitcoin. Virtually everyone who uses bitcoin does this to use it as a store of value. It serves well as a store of value since it is indestructible and highly portable. Bitcoin itself can never be lost (but codes to access them can). Since its inception, bitcoin has performed better than any other store of value on average, and today it is easily exchanged on online exchanges for other currencies.

If we take a step back and look at bitcoin, there is no denying that it is in many ways a success, but from a monetary perspective, it does not have high utility. It only really fulfills one of the key functions of money well and is only legal tender in two economically insignificant countries. The money dynamic identified previously is, therefore, not particularly powerful and has not historically been the key driver for bitcoin's success.

Scarcity and Store of Value

On August 27, 2010, Satoshi wrote the following on the Bitcoin Forum:

> *I think the traditional qualifications for money were written with the assumption that there are so many competing objects in the world that are scarce, an object with the automatic bootstrap of intrinsic value will surely win out over these without intrinsic value. But if there were nothing in the world with intrinsic value that could be used as money, only scarce but no intrinsic value, I think people would still take up something. (I'm using the word scarce here to only mean limited potential supply).*

This shows that Satoshi thought that scarcity was the key to value for Bitcoin and understood that limiting the supply is important. In Bitcoin, this is secured by the fixed number and successive halving of the amount of bitcoins released into circulation. Our analysis shows that it is not the scarcity that secures the value of bitcoin. In fact, if Bitcoin were too scarce, it would lower its utility because there would be no liquid market for it. That would undermine it as a store of value, which is its key function. Rather it is the supply dynamic we identified previously that explains this. As Satoshi wrote, it is controlling the supply and, thereby, the stock-to-flow ratio that underpins the value of bitcoin. Bitcoin is the only major currency whose monetary policy is not just set in stone but committed to code. The diminishing creation rate of bitcoin will ensure that all else being equal, the value of a unit will continue to rise due to the extraction dynamic identified previously.

Pump and Dump

In the last ten years, bitcoin has gone from around a hundred dollars to around 30,000 dollars as I write this. In October 2021, it was even double that, which is an astonishing three-hundred-fold increase over a decade but with steep drops of around 50–70% on five occasions in the same span. This effect is due to the bubble dynamic.

We can now see why bitcoin is susceptible to the positive reinforcement loop from unit value to store of value compared with other currencies. Bitcoin is unique in that its ability to store or, indeed, generate value is the primary function of its utility. As we saw previously, it performs badly as money since the money dynamic is weak. Almost the entire utility hinges on it being perceived as a store of value. When that happens, it is a self-reinforcing process. The dynamic is familiar for anyone following bitcoin: bitcoin price goes up. More people buy Bitcoin because it is a good store of value. The price increases the more and more people buy it until they don't. When the price stagnates or fails, the opposite happens because this is a reinforcing loop: the price goes down, and people start to sell, which makes the price go down further, which makes even more people sell.

Other currencies derive their utility primarily from other factors of the money dynamic and are thus not as volatile. Even the much-dreaded fiat currencies have a high base utility since they are legal tender. They also fulfill well all three functions of money: you can actually go to the store and buy groceries for it. Even if all stores took bitcoin, there would still be the basic necessity to pay your taxes. Fiat currencies, all their other weaknesses notwithstanding, have a much more powerful money dynamic.

A Sketch of Bitcoin as a Dynamic System

We can go into even greater detail to understand how the different components of Bitcoin relate to each other and produce the dynamics observed. It is evident that bitcoin has seen an explosive surge in value and is extremely volatile on a scale that no other currency or asset has matched since the inception of Bitcoin in 2009.

We can now recast the dynamics of Bitcoin according to the preceding dynamics. In the beginning, bitcoin was seeing a technical maturation phase where it was nothing more than a curiosity known by very few people and used by even fewer. In fact, it was not until halfway through 2010 that anyone used it for monetary purposes. Initial attempts were to promote it by exchanging bitcoin for dollars for it to serve as a store of value. None were successful since the money dynamic was completely absent. Without this dynamic to give it some utility, it was a mere abstract ideological project than any real monetary system. Had things continued like this, it would be hard to believe that we would be talking much about it today. It would have joined the already long list of failed virtual currencies. But instead, Bitcoin found its killer app: Silk Road. Ross Ulbricht created Silk Road as a dark net website for dealing in drugs and other illicit ware, and the currency of choice was none other than bitcoin. Being untraceable and swift, it suited this type of exchange well. Since there were already exchanges in a place like mtgox and BitInstant that allowed people to exchange bitcoin, it allowed bitcoin to gain a growing initial utility as a means of exchange. This initial boost from the money dynamic kickstarted a chain reaction.

In the analysis presented here, the success of Bitcoin can be understood as the interaction of the bubble dynamic and the supply dynamic constrained by the extraction dynamic. After the initial boost by the money dynamic, these together account for the continuous rise in the value of bitcoin. The extraction dynamic with its limited reserves and fixed schedule constrains the supply dynamic, which makes sure that the stock-to-flow ratio is high, thereby increasing the value of a unit. The bubble dynamic amplifies this effect through a reinforcing loop.

The extreme volatility can be explained by the weakness of the money dynamic, or to put it bluntly, the comparable uselessness of bitcoin as money outside the more nefarious niches of the economy. Other asset bubbles have a backstop since they usually have a basic utility that forms a base against which it will have some value. Bitcoin is, and Satoshi recognized this as we saw in the preceding quote, inherently worthless. It only gets its value from the scarcity with which new units are created.

This analysis also allows us to extrapolate future dynamics. As long as bitcoin's utility is primarily derived from its function as a store of value, it will continue to be volatile. If bitcoin was to improve the other monetary functions, unit of account and medium of exchange, it would stabilize and probably increase its value. Not until bitcoin is adopted for other purposes will its volatility end. This is where we need to consider the difference between a bitcoin standard and a gold standard.

Often, as in Ammous's *The Bitcoin Standard*, Bitcoin is portrayed as a store of value that could replace gold. This idea has been influential in the history of virtual currencies. Many of the most successful virtual currencies prior to bitcoin were backed by gold like e-gold. Nick Szabo presented the idea of Bitgold that in many ways resembled what would become bitcoin. The thought seems tempting and is supported by the same dynamic. Most people and companies do not buy gold physically but through instruments like ETFs, which are just virtual transactions through a brokerage account. The switch, therefore, seems simple and straightforward.

The difference is that somewhere in this virtual line is real physical gold, and gold, like currency, has utility beyond serving as a store of value. In fact, its primary utility is as jewelry and industrial applications. Consequently, there is a constant demand apart from its use as a store of value. This is not the case for bitcoin, which has no utility beyond its monetary utility. Although gold's price can also fluctuate, it is not as volatile. In the last ten years, gold rose around 70–80%, which is significantly less than bitcoin's 3000%, but unlike bitcoin, it had no drops of more than 30%. It, therefore, does not seem that bitcoin currently is able to match gold as a store of value even if it has been far superior as an object of speculation.

But the strength of bitcoin, unlike gold, is that the marginal cost of mining one bitcoin varies with the value of one unit. This is because the difficulty that determines the cost of mining depends on the total hash rate of the Bitcoin network. If the value drops and mining becomes unprofitable where electricity prices are highest, these miners will drop off the Bitcoin network. This will lower the hash rate and the marginal cost of mining a unit. This bodes well for Bitcoin as a system. It will probably always be profitable for someone to mine bitcoin. The Bitcoin dynamic system thus has a balancing loop between supply and extraction costs. If bitcoin drops 95%, it could still be profitable to mine it, since most miners will leave resulting in a drop in hash rate, which will make mining cheaper. Contrast this with gold or any other commodity that can be extracted or produced. If gold dropped by 95%, nobody would mine gold anymore, since it would not be profitable. The cost of mining gold would not fall along with the price of gold. There is no balancing loop between unit value and extraction cost for gold.

This, I believe, is what is truly unique for Bitcoin. There has never in the history of humanity been a type of money where the extraction cost increased and decreased with the value of the asset. Extraction costs are usually decoupled. Even if innovation that can lower the extraction costs is furthered by high asset prices, the reverse is not true. Indeed the variation seems to go the opposite way. If value goes up, innovation will make extraction costs go down. If value goes down, extraction costs may remain stable or go up. For metals and commodities, it seems like there is instead a weak reinforcing loop between value and marginal cost.

It thus seems likely that Bitcoin will remain volatile but also operational in the foreseeable future. Whether additional use cases can be added and Bitcoin expands its reach to other areas of society and the economy will be the topic of the next chapters.

CHAPTER 9

Social Organization

Bitcoin cannot be compared to any other currency in our contemporary world with respect to the social engagement it elicits. Nobody is tweeting incessantly about the Moroccan dirham or engaging in passionate defenses of the Vietnamese dong. Nobody goes to conferences where the theme is the Swedish krona, and nobody lifts a finger to divine the future of the Brunei dollar.

Contrast this with bitcoin, where a substantial subculture has developed that promotes it in every way on social media and creates software to improve its function. All of this is done for free without any direct remuneration. Bitcoin is the product of and attracts a special kind of social organization. The ideas about a cryptographically secure and private currency grew from specific social groups. In this chapter, we will focus on the different social groups and movements that played a significant part in developing a cryptographic virtual currency that would result in Bitcoin.

Hackers and the Origin of Open Source

In the 1970s, the counterculture movement in America also impacted computing. Before the 1970s, the government and big business dominated virtually everything related to hardware and software. Before that time, the government, mainly DARPA, had been a driving force in almost everything technology-related. DARPA directly or indirectly funded the most significant technological innovations in the post-war period.

© Anders Lisdorf 2023
A. Lisdorf, *Still Searching for Satoshi*, https://doi.org/10.1007/978-1-4842-9639-4_9

That started to change around 1970. Before this time, the typical developer had been an engineer or mathematician hired out of college by IBM or a similar corporation. Suddenly, young computer science graduates with different mindsets started looking for work. They were influenced by the counterculture and talked about freedom and justice. This, coupled with the Silicon Valley DIY approach, was the mold of the original hacker. Today the term has a more negative connotation of someone illicitly breaking into systems and stealing money or private data. The first part is similar to the original hackers. They also "broke into" systems, but they did it partly out of curiosity and partly out of a dislike of big business and their proprietary intellectual property. The slogan was that information wants to be free and software wants to be free, not proprietary, guarded by big corporations.

This ethos fueled the famous Homebrew Computer Club, where hobbyists built their own computers. Steve Wozniak was a part of this, and he managed to assemble and make the first Apple computer and its operating system. He did this from parts that became commercially available to hobbyists and by learning from his peers in the Homebrew Computer Club.

The hacker ethos also drove other developers to reverse engineer and hack other systems to create alternative versions or just to gain control of them. These projects were done in the spirit of the time, which was egalitarian and cooperative. Together hackers built software that would be shared freely with everyone else. This was the beginning of what would become open source development.

Open source refers to the software's source code being open for inspection by anyone. This contrasts with proprietary software developed by corporations, which is intellectual property guarded with secrecy by the rights holder.

The general principle of open source is that a loose group of volunteer developers work on a project and continuously release new versions to the public. The source code is also released to the public for inspection and for anyone else to tweak and further develop it.

These groups and how they work together can be structured differently. Nadia Eghbal has distinguished four general types of open source software projects based on research and her years of work at GitHub.

Eghbal constructs a typology along two dimensions: user growth and contributor growth (Table 9-1).

Table 9-1. *Types of open source projects*

	High User Growth	Low User Growth
High Contributor Growth	Federations (e.g., Linux)	Clubs (e.g., Astropy)
Low Contributor Growth	Stadiums (e.g., Babel)	Toys (e.g., SSH-chat)

Federations are how we typically think of open source projects with a thriving user base and developer community all working together to improve the software. Projects such as Rust, Node.js, and Linux fall into this category. But they are rare in real life. Instead, they resemble NGOs and are challenging to manage from a governance perspective.

Clubs are projects where most contributors are also users themselves. They are similar to meetups or hobby groups. That means that they attract dedicated participants but have a comparatively low reach. An example is Astropy, a collection of software packages written in Python used for astronomical purposes.

Toys are projects with low contributor and user growth. They are closer to personal projects and are often side projects of programmers. They are usually meant to be only for fun, often with no straightforward application. An example is SSH-chat, a project that uses the Secure Shell (SSH) protocol to provide a client meant for chat. This provides encrypted chat functionality, which seems convenient, but so does WhatsApp.

The last category is stadiums. They are projects where the user growth is high but not followed by a corresponding contributor growth as in federations. An example of this is Babel.js, a JavaScript compiler.

In a stadium, one or a few people make decisions on behalf of a large user base. This model is becoming more common today. The maintainers are proprietors through which everyone in the community is related. Other examples of such communities are hotels where everyone is connected through the central proprietor, the hotel owner.

Of these types, Bitcoin is today a stadium. Bitcoin has only five developers at its core who make decisions surrounding Bitcoin and many thousands of users who deploy the Bitcoin software without participating in any way in the development and maintenance of it.

Open source communities can go through different phases where they fit other categories. Initially, Bitcoin was a toy, essentially a side project for Satoshi, who first got the help of Hal Finney. Then Martti Malmi and Gavin Andresen joined and helped to work on the code. After Satoshi left, Andresen was left in charge. Throughout Bitcoin's history, a small core group has had a firm grip on what would go into the source code. That does not mean they could just build whatever they wanted because any change to Bitcoin depends on the willingness of the Bitcoin miners to adopt the new version of the software. Technically only the core group has the rights to change the Bitcoin source code. That means while anyone is free to develop new features, they cannot commit changes to the source code of the next version without being approved by someone from the core group.

There have been some heated debates about proposed changes to how Bitcoin should work since it has developed a lot since its original implementation, and there are diverging philosophies among the Bitcoin community. When such differences could not be resolved, this has resulted in splintering, as the example of Bitcoin Cash shows. In 2017 a debate around the future of Bitcoin resulted in a so-called hard fork, where Bitcoin split up in two: traditional Bitcoin and Bitcoin Cash. These two are now both available at exchanges with each their own ardent followers.

Cypherpunks

Another group that had a significant impact on the development of Bitcoin was the so-called cypherpunks. The cypherpunks were a group of people advocating using cryptography to effect social and political change. The word is a contraction of *cipher* and *cyberpunk*. *Cyberpunk* was made famous in William Gibson's 1984 novel *Neuromancer* depicting a dystopian future world that features marginalized persons who live with technological enhancements of their bodies. In this world, hackers fight the system or just whoever they are paid to. The word *cipher* comes from cryptography, where the cipher is an algorithm used for encryption. The difference between this group and the other hackers is that whereas hackers are usually left-leaning, cypherpunks derive their political orientation from libertarianism.

In 1992 Eric Hughes, Timothy C. May, and John Gilmore founded a group that started to meet regularly to discuss a wide range of themes such as politics, computer science, cryptography, and mathematics. There were ideological precursors to this movement, most notably David Chaum and his paper "Security Without Identification: Transaction Systems to Make Big Brother Obsolete" from 1985, which served as inspiration. Other inspirations were Ayn Rand and Verner Vinge's science fiction.

The same year a mailing list was established known as the cypherpunk mailing list. On this list, the cypherpunks debated an extended range of subjects from current political issues over grand visions of the future to complex cryptographic problems. The group was thus primarily connected through mailing lists where anonymous people communicated with no face-to-face interaction. This often resulted in a toxic environment of heated exchanges and, in agreement with the group's ideals, no moderation was done. Eventually, this led the list to implode in sectarian debates. It split up into other mailing lists with many of the same people. Different iterations existed at different times. The most important is the cryptography mailing list, where Satoshi posted his idea about Bitcoin.

145

Whereas the primary purpose of the open source community was to collaborate to build new free software, any actual group effort among the cypherpunks seems more incidental. Hal Finney, in an interview, was blunt enough to admit that other members of the community often quickly torpedoed most ideas, and Bitcoin was no exception.

That does not mean they did not cooperate as Hal Finney did with Satoshi. The community seems to have been more about exchanging ideas than collaborating on building code together. Wei Dai and Adam Back are good examples of this. Dai never built any code for his B-money idea, nor did he consider it. Dai described an idea to the community. Back also did this when he presented Hashcash, but he went on to build the code. It is telling, however, that he did so by himself. The same was the case for Satoshi. Bitcoin became an open source project only after its release. Seen from the outside, the cypherpunks seem more like a flock of lone wolfs than a coherent political movement.

The one thing that united the cypherpunks and ran through the emails on the cryptography mailing list was the distrust of the government. This is, of course, a common American trope, but in this modern version, the complete absence of government seems to be the dream. The first step is focusing on privacy, which naturally lies at the heart of cryptography. Through cryptography, the individual can secure privacy and escape the government completely. Apart from this, there is little that the cypherpunks all agree on.

The ideal vision of society for the cypherpunks is one of freedom from government interference. In the words of Timothy May, people live in "virtual regions," where individuals can make their own consensual transactions without any central entities, be it government or central banks, making rules for people to live by. The feeling was that the rules were unfair to the individual because they prioritized government and central control. In this decentralized mode, individuals can form small groups for particular purposes, but everything is transactional rather than rule-based. There should be no rules because rules are the way of government. In fact, there should be no ethics, either.

One of the founders of the cypherpunk movement, Eric Hughes, put the cypherpunk spirit in an often-cited slogan "Cypherpunks write code." Consequently, the only truth that needed to exist was the one embedded in the code. There are no moral points or ethics beyond that. If the code is faulty or you misused it or you were the subject of a hack, that is your problem only. It is your responsibility to understand and use the code correctly. Conversely, if someone used the code to obtain a result they are not entitled to, in the view of the surrounding society, say, access to government information, that is not their problem but those of who made the code that allowed them to gain access. The truth is in the code.

The cypherpunks were thus characterized by highly diverging beliefs but a common sentiment that revolves around freedom from government and rules and the right to privacy. As a movement, joint actions are ad hoc and uncoordinated.

Libertarians and Austrian Economics

The political philosophy of libertarianism originated from left-wing anti-authoritarian and anti-state sentiment, which it shared with anarchism. There are various schools of libertarianism, but they all share the value of liberty as the central value. They seek to minimize the encroachment of the state on individual freedom and are skeptical of authorities and other coercive social institutions. Apart from this, there is great variance of what it means to be a libertarian among libertarians themselves.

Two major groups differ significantly: left-libertarians and right-libertarians. The left-libertarians think the earth's resources should be distributed equally among all inhabitants without individual ownership. Therefore, they distrust capitalism in general. Right-libertarianism is the complete opposite in this respect and accepts only the institutions that guard the right of ownership and autonomy. This type of libertarianism developed from the so-called Austrian School of Economy and is the most common type of libertarianism in the United States.

The Austrian School of Economy is a school of thought emphasizing radical free market politics and individualism. Particularly Friedrich Hayek and Ludwig von Mises came to define the thinking of the Austrian school. The core belief was that social phenomena derived from the actions and perceptions of the individual. Therefore, markets should be wholly free, and government intervention should be abandoned entirely or minimized. When this is done, price formation automatically allocates resources to where they do the most good for society.

Concerning the Bitcoin community, it is naturally only the right-libertarians that are relevant. The libertarians in the United States had already adopted the idea of virtual currencies early on. The Liberty dollar and e-gold were founded by libertarians and promoted in the libertarian community. This fertilized the ground for Bitcoin.

The Social Structure of Bitcoin

One can say that Bitcoin was imagined by cypherpunks, built and maintained by open source hackers, and adopted by libertarians. These are the three main social groupings that affected the development of Bitcoin. Bitcoin is the product and medium of these groups and, therefore, intimately connected with their preferences and priorities.

There is no drive toward building a sizeable coherent movement to change society. None of them care deeply about what others think, even if they do like to argue their own opinion and ridicule each other. Group cohesion is limited and tied together by only a minimal set of beliefs and practices. Group cohesion is weak in another way since different splinter groups formed in the Bitcoin community, not to speak of the plethora of alternative cryptocurrencies that have been built subsequently in parallel with Bitcoin by people who disagreed with certain features of Bitcoin.

There is a general dislike of bureaucracy and moral reasoning. For example, if you sent money to the wrong account, you lost your private key, or someone found a loophole in the code to create new bitcoin, so what? Hard-liners do not think this is a problem. The truth is in the code, and if you were careless enough to send money to the wrong account or lost your private key, that is your problem. Suppose somebody found a way to create new bitcoin outside the mining process; good for them. All of these things happened with Bitcoin. Rather than a general principled moral-based reasoning, there is a preference for a transactional view. The transaction is metaphorically, and also quite literally, all there is. The Bitcoin blockchain is a list of transactions. No one knows or cares what those transactions were or whether they were donations, investments, or payments for pizza, guns, or ransom.

Grid/Group Characterization

One way to make sense of this is to consult anthropological theory. One of the key ideas of the grandfather of sociology, Emile Durkheim, was that any given system of classification is a product of its social relations. Ideas are formed by the social organization that produced them. But how may we make sense of the relationship between the social organization of the Bitcoin community and their ideas?

The British anthropologist Mary Douglas has expanded the fundamental Durkheimian insight into a tool to conceptualize the relationship between cosmological ideas and social relations. She observes that one dimension concerns the "group," that is, the extent to which the group exerts power over the individual or the individual exerts power itself. The other dimension is what she calls grid and describes the extent to which ideas about the world are shared. These two dimensions are laid out on two axes. The x-axis concerns the group dimension. 0 is where no forces are exerted on the individual. Moving right increases the pressure exerted on the individual by the group to comply with rules and conventions. Shifting left means that the individual increasingly exerts their own pressure on the surroundings. The y-axis is the so-called "grid" dimension describing the degree to which ideas are shared in society. The grid dimension thus measures the extent of a public system of classification that determines the individual in the cosmos. Above 0 is the area of shared public classifications. Going down this axis just above and below the x-axis are increasingly marginal and fringe groups of society. At the bottom of the vertical dimension are private ideas no one shares. This is the so-called group/grid model that Douglas developed in her book *Natural Symbols*, which can be used to conceptualize different social groups and their ideas about the world.

According to Douglas, the top-right quadrant with a strong group and strong grid promotes "(...) a routinized piety towards authority and its symbols, beliefs in a punishing, moral universe, and a category of rejects. Any bureaucratic system which is sufficiently secure and insulated from criticism will tend to think the same way. This is the monastic life, or the military society." This is also a description that fits most modern Western societies. Modern nation-states are characterized by a requirement for the individual to be subject to the state's authority. The state has a monopoly of power. This is government, and the banking system is just an extension of this general mode of living with its bureaucracy and rules.

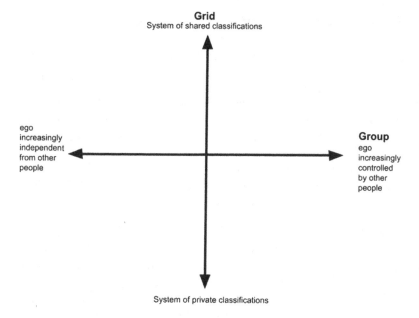

Figure 9-1. *Group and grid classification*

Contrast this with the description of the lower-left quadrant where we find the "voluntary outcastes, tramps, gypsies, rich eccentrics, or others who retain their freedom at a cost" as Mary Douglas writes in *Natural Symbols*. It is hard not to recognize the different social groups we have viewed here as fitting this description. They agree little with the surrounding majority society of the modern nation-state, and there are only a few shared beliefs among themselves. Furthermore, they are voluntary outcasts and eccentrics. This applies whether we are considering the libertarians, the hackers, the cypherpunks, or the Bitcoin community with only minor differences in the distance to the center of the grid.

Bitcoin, Society, and the Cosmos

In summary, we can see that Bitcoin was imagined by the extropians, created by cypherpunks, developed by open source hackers, and adopted by libertarians. It depends on a particular type of social organization characterized by weak grid and weak group. There is no great degree of cohesion between the members of the community. Engagement is transactional. Compare this with the surrounding world of fiat currencies with general rules, regulations, and elaborate bureaucratic processes.

Douglas summarizes the difference between the two modes: "The line across the page separates the area of conformity from innovation." This can be seen in the monetary instruments they use. Fiat currencies follow the way of conformity, while Bitcoin is the innovation. As such, the currencies act as both instruments of and proxies for the different types of social and cosmological orientations embedded in the social groups.

Bitcoin is much more than a fascinating technological innovation. It is deeply embedded in the social structures by which it was created and the product of these social structures. These social structures also promote a particular view of the world that differs radically from the way of the surrounding society. They try to push back on these and change them through subversive acts and overt propaganda. So there is more at stake than just a currency; it is about the ideal shape of society and the world in general.

CHAPTER 10

Religion

To many people, Bitcoin is much more than just a convenient online payment option or a way to make money speculating on its continued rise in value. It is a cause to which some people dedicate themselves with considerable zeal. That this is something more than an ordinary interest of technology enthusiasts, I have felt myself. Whenever I have written something in public that could be interpreted as critical to Bitcoin, I have invariably been faced with the wrath of Bitcoin enthusiasts calling me things that do not need quoting. One interesting example that is from a response to an answer I gave a few years back about Bitcoin on Quora comes here:

> *Heretic. You will be forced to eat your word once BTC crosses $10 million, solves world hunger, and brings peace to middle-east. Once each terror attack is logged into the blockchain everyone will be secure because crypto.*
>
> —User Kamran Khan

Having written and debated about tech for decades, this is something I have never experienced. Usually, the responses to my articles and posts are a shrug or helpful clarifications from detail-oriented conscientious readers or even heated counterarguments. Still, this is the first time I have been called a heretic for writing critically about anything tech related.

Some people call themselves Bitcoin maximalists and believe it is the only true and fair currency in the world. Some people, like the Quora user

© Anders Lisdorf 2023
A. Lisdorf, *Still Searching for Satoshi*, https://doi.org/10.1007/978-1-4842-9639-4_10

quoted, believe Bitcoin will transform the world. Some of this enthusiasm for Bitcoin approaches religious zeal. Indeed some aspects of Bitcoin do resemble religion quite closely.

What Is Religion?

Religion comes in many different forms and shapes. If religion were only world religions such as Christianity, Buddhism, or Hinduism, it would be nonsensical to compare Bitcoin to them. There is no agreed definition of what the essence of religion is. This is not for lack of trying. For decades discussions have been made about the definition of religion. We do not, however, need a full-fledged definition of religion but rather to accept that there are multiple distinct aspects of religion. Some of these we find around Bitcoin too.

A religion always has a community of believers or followers. This I will call the Bitcoin community. They engage with each other, share similar ideas about the world, and have a shared goal. We are not claiming that Bitcoin is a god or divine as such, but rather that religious behavior and ideas have shaped the reception and formation of the Bitcoin community in multiple ways.

The Prophet

See how the faithful city
has become a prostitute!
She once was full of justice;
righteousness used to dwell in her—
but now murderers!
Your silver has become dross,
your choice wine is diluted with water.

Your rulers are rebels,

partners with thieves;

they all love bribes

and chase after gifts.

They do not defend the cause of the fatherless;

the widow's case does not come before them.

Therefore the Lord, the Lord Almighty,

the Mighty One of Israel, declares:

"Ah! I will vent my wrath on my foes

and avenge myself on my enemies.

I will turn my hand against you;

I will thoroughly purge away your dross

and remove all your impurities.

I will restore your leaders as in days of old,

your rulers as at the beginning.

Afterward you will be called

the City of Righteousness,

the Faithful City."

Zion will be delivered with justice,

her penitent ones with righteousness.

But rebels and sinners will both be broken,

and those who forsake the Lord will perish.

—Book of Isaiah 1:21–28 (translation:
New International Version)

The prophet Isaiah is believed to have lived in ancient Israel in the eighth century BCE. Since sources are naturally sparse, nothing much is known with certainty. Some assume that he came from an aristocratic class. Still, he had intimate knowledge of the conditions of poor, homeless, and landless people indicating that he was not a traditional aristocrat. It is also vital to notice that he was not of a priestly family. This puts him outside the formal religious authority with sympathy for the victimized and oppressed.

Religions often feature the figure of the prophet. This is particularly prevalent in the Abrahamic religions (Judaism, Christianity, and Islam), where it is a central focus. The figure of the prophet is someone who has hidden knowledge about the actual state of the world, particularly about the future. There is often resentment of the present society, its mores, and its general decay. In the Abrahamic religions, the prophet commands people to return to the way of God and the proper ethical way of living.

This diagnosis of present society as a fallen society is supplied with a prescription for the right way of living. In Islam, they include the five daily prayers, the Hajj, and the study of the Quran, among others; in Christianity, the Golden Rule.

The prophet usually lives at the fringes of society. In the Old Testament, it is the desert. He does not come from the mainstream of religious authority. It is precisely the fact that the prophet comes from outside the established power structures that makes the prophecy powerful. Consequently, the established power often targets the prophet, which adds to the moral indignation fueling the prophecy.

As a person, the prophet is enigmatic and charismatic, drawing followers due to his/her ability to capture their attention and convince them of his/her worldview. In addition, he/she is a good orator and able to put thoughts into precise and memorable quotes that his followers are able to remember and live by.

In Bitcoin, the "prophet" is, of course, Satoshi Nakamoto. He is the enigmatic founder whose origin, if not quite divine, is then unknown. He travels in arcane knowledge, that is, cryptography. Satoshi's worldview is one where the established world order is depraved due to excessive lending by governments and banks, resulting in credit bubbles, where the undeserving banks have to be bailed out.

According to Satoshi, the government runs the monetary system and is perceived as having become morally corrupt (cf. "See how the faithful city/has become a prostitute!/She once was full of justice;/ righteousness used to dwell in her"). Central banks are printing too much money, which leads to inflation (cf. "Your silver has become dross/your choice wine is diluted with water"). Inflation, according to Satoshi, effectively steals money from ordinary people. Furthermore, the financial institutions are corrupt since, as trusted third parties, they do not ensure that transactions are non-reversible since they mediate disputes and decide the outcome (cf. "Your rulers are rebels/partners with thieves/they all love bribes/and chase after gifts"). This increases the price of transactions and makes it too high for simple payments. Since transactions are not anonymous, they also take away peoples' right to privacy since it is possible to trace each transaction of the individual. This allows the government to snoop on private affairs (cf. "They do not defend the cause of the fatherless/the widow's case does not come before them"). All this is unethical and unfair.

In opposition to this, Satoshi has devised an alternative monetary system, Bitcoin, that runs completely independent of the evil central government. Unlike fiat currencies, Bitcoin is free to use and completely private. It is not inflationary; quite the contrary, it prints less and less money over time until, eventually, all has been printed. This leads to deflation, which will increase the value of Bitcoin.

Satoshi predicts a future where the existing financial institutions are no longer needed and payments are free and completely private. There will be no more credit bubbles, and people who want to save their money will see them increase in value. Satoshi seems to be echoing Isaiah:

I will turn my hand against you

I will thoroughly purge away your dross

and remove all your impurities

will restore your leaders as in days of old

your rulers as at the beginning

Afterward you will be called

the City of Righteousness

the Faithful City

Zion will be delivered with justice

her penitent ones with righteousness

But rebels and sinners will both be broken

and those who forsake the Lord will perish.

Satoshi is, like other prophets, also from the fringes though not literally in a geographical sense. London is hardly a desert. But he is from the fringes of finance, that is, not a banker or economist but a computer scientist who specializes in cryptography. Therefore, he has no connection to or affiliation with the existing banking system. His prose is unusually clear, even crisp, compared with his peers on the cryptography mailing list, and he has a way of formulating ideas that captivate people.

Satoshi's character is, therefore, somewhat similar to a prophet in the Abrahamic religions. These qualities help explain why he, unlike any of the other virtual currency founders we have reviewed, was able to build a following and turn it into a thriving community. Wei Dai, for example, had many similar ideas but was not able to explain them in the same way. Likewise, David Chaum built a virtual currency that did much of what Bitcoin does, but he did not have Satoshi's prophetic qualities.

Scriptures

Avalokita, the Holy Lord and Bodhisattva, was moving in the deep course of the Wisdom which has gone beyond. He looked down from on high, He beheld but five heaps, and He saw that in their own-being they were empty. Here, O Sariputra, form is emptiness and the very emptiness is form ; emptiness does not differ from form, form does not differ from emptiness, whatever is emptiness, that is form, the same is true of feelings, perceptions, impulses, and consciousness.

—The Heart Sutra (translation: E. Conze)

The Heart Sutra is one of the most famous sacred texts of Buddhism. Several commentaries exist dating back to the eighth or ninth century. Today it is one of the most commonly used texts of Buddhism.

In religions where dogma and teachings are essential, sacred scriptures have a central role to play. We know these holy texts from world religions such as the Vedas of Hinduism; the Torah, Bible, and Quran of the Abrahamic faiths; as well as the Tripitaka of Buddhism. They feature heavily in civilizations where a social class can devote themselves to bureaucratic concerns, that is, where the division of labor in society allows a type of people to pursue other work than the manual labor required for survival. Religious texts are among the first things such cultures write down when they acquire the skill of writing.

The sacred texts are a particular type of text since they are attributed special significance. Historically, these scriptures have been designated as focal texts in their specific culture. This is, for example, how the Gospel was established as a sacred text from several different texts circulated in the third and fourth centuries CE. These focal texts have a unique quality to them that is beyond reproach, a revealed truth, if not directly from God, then divinely inspired.

In connection with these is another class of texts consisting of commentaries, sayings, aphorisms, or hymns that are secondary but related to the focal text. They are not entirely revealed truth but can be tied to the same source of truth. They serve to expand the scope of the teachings of the focal text. In the Judaic tradition, this includes the Mishnah and Talmud.

For Bitcoin, we find a similar structure. Though not quite trafficking in divine revelations, Satoshi, as the designated "prophet," has produced the Bitcoin whitepaper as the focal text of Bitcoin. In discussions around Bitcoin, this text is beyond reproach in much the same manner as sacred scripture. There is no discussion of whether this was right or wrong or debate as is usual with academic papers. Instead, it is used as an ultimate source of truth in arguments.

Along with this are the thousands of words of Satoshi written on the Bitcoin Forum. These also have a special status since it is possible to expand the scope of Satoshi's vision beyond that written explicitly in the Bitcoin whitepaper. The last group is the emails purportedly from Satoshi, released years after by the recipients of these emails. The fact that Satoshi withdrew from the public and left a finite body of text helps establish this structure. These texts are even published as a book in the fashion of the New Testament by Phil Champagne entitled *The Book of Satoshi*.

It is interesting to contrast the situation with other virtual currencies. For example, David Chaum wrote a paper very similar to the Bitcoin whitepaper describing his vision for a future virtual currency. This is entitled "Blind Signatures for Untraceable Payments," published in 1982. Looking through this, it has many features that resemble the Bitcoin whitepaper. So many, in fact, that it would be reasonable to assume it was the direct inspiration. Nevertheless, Chaum's paper never gained a following. It is, therefore, likely that the texts produced by Satoshi, fitting a structure known from religious scripture, helped focus the vision of Bitcoin in much the same way as religious texts do with religious visions.

Cargo Cults

At the beginning of the 1940s, American forces were stationed at what was then called the New Hebrides, current-day Vanuatu. With them, they brought immense amounts of cargo. Thousands of the natives worked for the Americans. After the war, when the Americans left Vanuatu, a local religious leader's followers built symbolic landing strips to bring cargo like they had seen the Americans get during the war. They instituted military parades where participants wore T-shirts painted with the letters USA. All of this to mimic the Americans they had witnessed bring vast amounts of cargo during the war.

The phenomenon of cargo cults originated in Melanesia in the late nineteenth century as a response to Western colonialism. The indigenous population of the Melanesian islands of the Pacific had experienced Western colonial administrators, missionaries, and plantation owners with their higher level of material wealth. With them came modern technology, clothes, and other goods. In Tok Pisin, the pidgin language of New Guinea, the word "cargo" means trade goods or supplies. This came more generally to represent wealth.

Cargo cults sought to attain the lifestyle and wealth of colonialism. They are characterized by an attempt to copy the behavior of Western colonialists to achieve the same level of material goods. Examples include building mock airstrips and marching like soldiers with sticks for rifles, as the indigenous population witnessed the soldiers of World War II do. The hope was that this would bring about a situation where the ancestors would bring similar wealth or the colonialists would share their wealth. While cargo cults originated and proliferated in Melanesia, they are documented worldwide, particularly in Africa and the Caribbean. This hints that the phenomenon is more than just a local cultural peculiarity but a cohesive feature of the modern world.

Bitcoin exhibits some of the same characteristics, albeit in a completely different context. For example, there are no indigenous people unless you count digital natives as such; there are no ancestors or rituals per se. Still, there are some robust structural similarities.

There is also a perceived antagonism to a materially and politically superior social organization: where cargo cults respond to Western colonialism, the Bitcoin community responds to the government and the banking system. These are considered oppressive and similarly perceived to enslave and take away personal freedom.

The people who devote themselves to Bitcoin in the Bitcoin community also copy this antagonism. They take their cues from investment bankers when they apply similar language and behavior. It is not uncommon to hear them talk about building a crypto portfolio consisting of different kinds of cryptocurrency like Litecoin, XRP, and Dogecoin alongside Bitcoin. These portfolios copy the portfolio approach in traditional investing, where risk is spread across several different securities to arrive at a more manageable risk profile. But traditional portfolio investing is based on securities with inherent value and real-world connections. A stock, for example, gives you fractional ownership rights of a company that produces something or has a demonstrable path to revenue. Commodities are physical and can be bought and sold on the market. Cryptocurrencies, with limited exceptions, have no connection to the real world or any inherent value. They mostly can't be used for the basic function of a currency: a medium of exchange. Dogecoin has no value other than as an object of speculation. But, of course, people may believe it really will be the currency on Mars, as Elon Musk suggested.

Still, no security would be allowed to be traded on such a tenuous promise in the traditional world of finance. The popular cryptocurrency XRP aims to be a more efficient cross-border payment solution. Still, it has yet to make any noticeable dent in the incumbents like Western Union's hold on the remittance industry. Litecoin is used for transfer between people, much like bitcoin but faster. Again, it is more the promise that it can do it than a unique real-world application since common applications like Zelle and Square provide such services to a vastly greater number of users. These examples are chosen because they are the most promising of the thousands of alternative cryptocurrencies and carry significant potential. But contrast this with stocks that already generate revenue and have a book value. It is not the same.

Self-proclaimed "analysts" set targets for bitcoin, again mirroring a common practice for securities like common stocks or commodities like gold. Targets for bitcoin will be, for example, $100,000 or, as Ark Invest's Cathie Wood has it, $1.48 million in 2030. These targets are either taken out of thin air or supported by only the haziest of analysis, which invariably boils down to what-if scenarios and wishful thinking. Naturally, traditional analysts in the world of finance also have some element of uncertainty, but they are constrained by requirements of documentation of how they arrive at these assumptions. With the exception of more mainstream investors like Ark Invest, most analysis pays only lip service to traditional finance methods.

Another area where the behavior of finance is mimicked is the application of technical analysis. Traders in the finance industry often use a technique called technical analysis, which in itself has been accused of being more magic than science. It relies on recognizing patterns in graphs of the value of traded equities. Basically, technical analysts believe that market movements are not entirely random and can be predicted by analyzing market data and applying various charting tools and technical indicators.

These practices resemble the cargo cults building landing strips, marching with mock rifles, and copying colonial mores. There is no relation between the original application of these behaviors, how they work, and their application in the cryptocurrency world. One might counter that it has worked since many have gotten extremely rich from bitcoin. But then again, this is not uncommon for early members of cults in general or Ponzi schemes. The success of a few or even many individuals in the short term is no proof.

We should also note that we only discuss structural behavior similarities across a diverse cryptocurrency community population. There are many exceptions to this, and bitcoin may yet become the future standard of value. Indeed that is what we will consider in the next chapter. It just currently has virtually no documented real-world use outside of its role as an object of speculation.

Millenarianism

In their book *Three Worlds, and the Harvest of This World* from 1877, Nelson H. Barbour and Charles Taze Russel claimed to have determined the time of Jesus's second coming to the earth to restore it to a paradise-like state. This they believed would be completed by 1878. When that did not happen, a new date was set. When that also did not happen, new dates continued to be set. This, of course, is the story of Jehovah's Witnesses, a Christian movement that opposed certain key Christian teachings like the Trinity and the existence of an immortal soul. It is one of the most successful types of religious or social movements called millenarianism.

Millenarianism is the belief in the imminent coming of a radically new constitution of the world that is qualitatively different and better. The impetus of these groups in Christian cultures can be traced to the passage in Revelation 20:1–10, where the imprisonment of the devil for a thousand years is foretold. The name *millenarianism* is thus derived from the Latin word for thousand: "mille." Millenarianist movements often perceive the existing society as unjust and believe in an imminent transformation of the world that will rid it of the current corrupt regime and install a new and better one.

This type of belief has influenced the history of Bitcoin in two ways. One is more mundane and the other more pervasive and subtle. For both of them, Bitcoin is not the end goal but the driver of the change. As we saw in the case of the similarity to cargo cults, it is not that Bitcoin by itself will bring wealth. Instead, Bitcoin is a critical ingredient in a more fundamental social or even cosmological change.

The World of the Bitcoin Standard

Among libertarians, the dream of the good old days of the gold standard in international monetary policy is a guiding light. The Bitcoin community has accepted this sentiment with the twist that bitcoin should be the new standard. The new world would see fiat currencies abandoned. Central banks and governments would no longer recklessly print money, effectively stealing it from ordinary people. Consider one answer on Quora that echoes this sentiment:

> *Maybe the current monitory system is doing good for some, but the question is where is the wealth people labored for years? Why is it in the hands of the few? Isn't it fraud to have these central banks, privately owned, print money and determine the value? What about the misery they cause, ranging from sanctioning countries or companies minding their own business to instigating wars? Who gave them that power to play God, to begin with? (...) Anywhere, it will be interesting to see how it goes but I am a firm believer banks must go. They are the world largest terrorist institutions the world have ever seen. The current fiat currency system is doing no good to the people of the entire world. Do you know how it sounds to have 7.6 billion people being held hostage by these banking cartels?*

> —User Emmanuel Bikorimana

With Bitcoin, this oppressive power of the government and banks would entirely vanish, and people live in virtual communities where they choose their peers individually, forming smaller interest-based communities. Individuals would be completely free to choose because the bitcoin standard would ensure complete predictability, and no one would be able to interfere with it.

With the new world of the bitcoin standard, individuals can be free. The people believing in this world often call themselves bitcoin maximalists and see themselves as digital nomadic tribes. With the coming of the new world order, they can live anywhere, and work and social interactions would take place online. The nation-states as we know them would no longer exist or be severely limited in their power. This is a pretty pedestrian change of the world as far as millenarian transformation goes.

The Singularity

The other way that millenarian thought has influenced Bitcoin is much more subtle but also pervasive. An argument could be made that Bitcoin would not exist without this current. This current is much more radical and even cosmic in its outlook. To understand it, we have to start in another place.

One of the greatest prophets of Silicon Valley is Ray Kurzweil. With his technological leadership and decades of writing, he has inspired and stimulated technologists everywhere. With his groundbreaking book *The Age of Spiritual Machines*, he connected the technological progress of the computer age with the prospect of ontological transformation. Based on the insight that technological progress seemed to follow an exponential rather than linear progress at some point, humanity would hit the Singularity, which in mathematics is a point where a function is undefined. On the other side of this point, the world would be transformed.

Humans would become post-humans. With neural implants, it would be possible to upload your mind to a completely virtual world of supercomputers and the Internet. It would even be possible to resurrect the dead and bring them back to life in this new world. This conviction is called transhumanism, which is the belief that humans will be able to overcome their limitations and transcend the human condition to become superhuman. While transhumanism is a fairly recent phenomenon driven in large part by the technological progress of the modern world, Meghan O'Gieblyn has shown the deep historical and religious roots of this movement. In her book *God, Human, Animal, Machine*, she investigates the roots of transhumanism.

Contrary to the transhumanists' own conviction that transhumanism is recent and can be traced back to Julian Huxley, who mentioned it for the first time in 1957, Peter Harrison and Joseph Wolyniak showed that the modern use of the word is attested for the first time in Huxley's 1952 lecture "Knowledge, Morality, and Destiny" but that it has a far deeper history. It is mentioned in Dante's "Divine Comedy" in book 9, where he invents a new Italian word, *transhumanar*, to describe the transformation that takes place of the human as he enters heaven. The word is translated to "transhuman" in Henry Francis Carrey's 1814 edition of the "Divine Comedy."

O'Gieblyn shows how the thoughts of Huxley are influenced by his personal friend, the French Jesuit priest Pierre Teilhard de Chardin. In a 1947 essay, he noticed how the invention of mass communication like TV and radio had created a global network of human minds, which he called the "noosphere." Progress would eventually lead to a dramatic transformation where a network of human machines would give way to an "'etherized' universal consciousness" that would span the globe. This would create an intelligence explosion, which he called the Omega Point that would enable humanity to "break through the material framework of time and space." The similarities between this vision and Kurzweil's singularity are evident.

In order to see how this vision is at all related to Bitcoin, we need to consider another small group of technological zealots that have also had an outsized impact on the development of virtual currencies in general and Bitcoin in particular, that is, the extropians.

The extropians were a loosely organized community participating in email lists, conferences, a magazine, and a foundation that never exceeded a few thousand. The name comes from the word *extropy*, which was first used as an antonym to *entropy* in a 1967 cryogenics paper. The term was later used to signify the transhuman potential. The Extropy Institute launched its email list in 1991 and began to promote conferences about transhumanism. The concept grew out of cryogenics, the purpose of which was to be able to be resuscitated at a later point in life when the world had been transformed. These cryogenically conserved people would be the dead that would be awoken at the time of the singularity. The extropians share the same transhuman convictions as Kurzweil, Nick Bostrom, and other prominent transhumanists.

This posed a problem. Since extropians knew they would not live long enough to experience the inflection point where humans and machines merged, they had to be cryogenically preserved until that day. But when you can't trust banks, and inflation is slowly eating away your funds over time, it becomes a problem how one could have funds left at this time. The alternative had to be an electronic virtual currency that existed outside the established banking industry. As Finn Brunton puts it in his *Digital Cash*: "The 'long, long term' time frame of investment and financial speculation is no longer a matter of planning your retirement and senescence but of arranging assets to transcend your life and ultimately money entirely."

Nick Szabo made predictions about the coming of such money at extropian events. In 1995 he predicted that by 1999 a million people would be using virtual currencies and the economy would reach a billion dollars by 2005. As we have seen earlier, Szabo had presented many of the ideas that would come together in Bitcoin, even if they arrived about ten years later than he had predicted. He thereby fertilized the ground for what would become Bitcoin along with other extropians on the cryptography mailing list.

Another extropian who would become even more instrumental in Bitcoin's creation was Hal Finney. He and his wife had been extropians from the beginning. He had also tried his own version of a virtual currency called reusable proof of work or RPOW. Without his interest in Bitcoin and assistance in the very beginning, Bitcoin might very well have slipped into oblivion. Hal Finney's singular importance is easily overlooked, perhaps due to the fact that he died much too early from ALS in 2014. In his book *Digital Cash: The Unknown Story of the Anarchists, Utopians, and Technologists Who Created Cryptocurrency*, Finn Brunton traces the origins of Bitcoin and identifies Finney as the real main character behind the advent of cryptocurrencies. He writes, "Hal Finney, who quietly became the main character of this book, died in 2014. His body was perfused, cooled below freezing, and placed in long-term storage in the Alcor cryonics facility" (p. 205). Fittingly this was partially funded by his bitcoin reserves. Finney thus embodies the creation of cryptocurrencies in body and mind.

The Coming of the Thousand-Year Reign

We can thus see the powerful impact millenarian ideas have had on the development of Bitcoin and cryptocurrencies. Humans have all days believed in an imminent radical transformation of the world even if the mode and result differ across cultures. Such beliefs bring about extraordinary motivation and the power of change.

Bitcoin was never just a convenient new way of making payments, like many other virtual currencies of its time. Instead, it was fueled by the belief in a fundamental, even radical, change of the world that would be imminent. This was an essential driver for the creation and adoption of this new virtual currency. Bitcoin was not necessarily seen as a magical technology that would bring about this new world but as a crucial component for it.

It may be that these deep millenarist convictions of Bitcoin proponents separated it from other virtual currencies like e-gold. In contrast to other virtual currencies at the time, Bitcoin was more than just a utility to its proponents; it was a necessity that would be crucial in transforming the world.

Bitcoin and Religion

Bitcoin is more than just another technical innovation to many people in the Bitcoin community. It clearly generates responses and fervor that far outpace even the most ardent Apple fanatic at the Apple Keynote event. These people feel deeply that this is the solution to the future and will bring them and other believers great wealth. The inventor is treated with a reverence worthy of a prophet, and his texts are still read and continue to inspire to this day.

There is no explicit reference to gods, spirits, or otherworldly creatures, but the appearance is structurally similar to other well-known religious phenomena. This could be an important clue as to why Bitcoin still, to this day, attracts so much attention and so many resources are invested into it. Past or present, none of the other virtual currencies exhibit similar features. The second greatest cryptocurrency, Ethereum, also commands a dedicated and energized following, but it does not have a single prophet-like figure or focal texts. It certainly does not elicit the same emotional statements when criticized.

Part of Bitcoin's success could be derived from the religious motivations it elicits in the Bitcoin community. As history has shown, such motivations can be important drivers of change.

CHAPTER 11

Future

Bitcoin was born from visions of the future and is today primarily driven by expectations of what it could be in the future:

> Bitcoin will hit $1,000,000.

> Bitcoin will replace gold as a safe harbor in investments.

> We will see a new Bitcoin standard emerge in place of fiat currencies.

These are common beliefs in the Bitcoin community. On the other hand, we have skeptics that are just as convinced that Bitcoin is nothing but a Ponzi scheme that, like all other Ponzi schemes, will fall at some point. The problem is that these views are rarely supported by any analysis beyond what-if thought experiments and subjective opinion. Either of these scenarios or some completely different ones may come true, but we should be able to do better.

In this chapter, we will use the insights we gained about Bitcoin in this book to understand how the future of Bitcoin might look. Like any statement about the future, it is based on assumptions. We will look at several possible scenarios that vary these assumptions and ascertain how they could develop and how Bitcoin would fit in. These scenarios are not exhaustive but are meant to suggest possible future trajectories based on current trends. They operate on different timescales with different assumptions of technological and historical development.

© Anders Lisdorf 2023
A. Lisdorf, *Still Searching for Satoshi*, https://doi.org/10.1007/978-1-4842-9639-4_11

The first two scenarios, "normalization" and "fringe consolidation," work from an assumption that we will continue within the limits of the known contemporary world. Governments persist, and people continue to live in nation-states with banks and the institutions we know today. The following two scenarios involve substantial societal changes and have a longer timeframe. The scenario "disappearance of the nation-state" assumes that the current dominance of nation-states ends. The "singularity" further assumes a radical change in technology. We follow the trajectory predicted by Ray Kurzweil. The final two scenarios involve a radical change of our society. The "post-apocalypse" scenario assumes a cataclysmic event's occurrence, while the last scenario, "interplanetary," considers what happens when humans colonize the solar system.

Normalization

In this scenario, Bitcoin adapts to the surrounding majority culture and becomes mainstream rather than a niche undertaking. For this to happen, several things need to happen.

The regulatory paradigm needs to improve. If bitcoin is to become a mainstream currency, several legal issues need to be resolved. It has more to do with clarity than lenience or austerity of regulation. We do see a drive toward this in multiple jurisdictions but are not quite there yet. One of the biggest problems is that it needs to be clarified precisely what bitcoin is legally and that this definition differs across countries and even internally in a country. The European Union, for example, has yet to pass specific regulations concerning Bitcoin. Consequently, old laws, often more than a hundred years old, are used locally in member countries to govern trade and taxation of bitcoin. In the United States, bitcoin is classified as currency, commodity, or property, depending on which government office you ask.

If the United States and European Union decided to accept bitcoin as a currency like any other and include it in existing anti-money laundering regulations, it would be a big step toward normalizing it. That would mean banks could start accepting and managing accounts in bitcoin on behalf of their customers. That could expand its use as a medium of exchange. Existing processes in the banking world for money transfer and clearance would be brought to bear on Bitcoin. That would open its usage up to people currently suspicious of or alienated from the bitcoin trade. In practice, banks would probably act like contemporary crypto exchanges and only transfer aggregated sums between them and manage internal transfers in internal accounts. That would minimize the total number of transactions on the blockchain.

In this scenario, everyone will use a digital wallet as the primary tool for economic transactions. It could be part of a new super app, built on existing solutions by digital payments providers or offered by specialized companies. In this app, you could seamlessly pay in cryptocurrency, fiat currency, or any other type of currency. There is no reason loyalty points should not be part of this too. Customers would be able to exchange bitcoin and cryptocurrencies seamlessly.

Through this app, the promise of Bitcoin as a way to provide global remittance services would come true. People in countries with high inflation and unstable political and banking systems could store their money in other currencies. Whether this would be bitcoin or stable coins pegged to fiat currencies depends on whether it can tame its volatility. People in third-world countries tend to be less engaged in ideological fights about fiat currencies' inflationary characteristics and more concerned with knowing that their savings are there next year when they plan to buy a house and not lost to the next bust cycle of Bitcoin.

The wallet could also be a new platform for legal and economic activities where ownership could be documented and transferred through sales. As establishing ownership as a smart contract in the digital wallet becomes more common, it starts to absorb certain types of ownership previously documented offline, especially digital ones. For example, stocks will probably remain within the banking system, but fractional stocks could be traded here. Similarly, ownership of other assets like houses would remain within the nationally accepted methods of documenting ownership except for the most progressive states, which are probably smaller ones. Here it would be possible to use a blockchain to register legal ownership.

This development would increase the attractiveness of bitcoin as a payment option for online and physical merchants due to an increased speed of settlement and presumably lower fees. In addition, it would probably be possible to dispute transactions, unlike the current state of affairs, since transactions would primarily happen off-chain in the banking system since most bitcoin payments are handled by the banking system rather than directly.

We saw in Chapter 8 how bitcoin's lack of essential utility, particularly as a medium of exchange and unit of account, was a primary reason for the volatility of bitcoin. In this scenario, the volatility is reduced since the essential utility is increased and the bitcoin price will rise steadily but not as dramatically as in the first 15 years.

That would see the exit of many of the original Bitcoin believers, who would think this new development an abomination. Another fork could be formed, or they would rally around Bitcoin Cash as the primary flavor of bitcoin, preserving the original founder's ideas. They would presumably try to evade much of the newfound regulation, and exchanges would move to other more leniently regulated localities.

Fringe Consolidation

In this scenario, the general public loses patience with Bitcoin. The boom and bust dynamic leads to one too many busts for the regular bitcoin investor, who by this time would primarily have memories of losing money on bitcoin because they, unlike the more sophisticated bitcoin traders, do not have the tools to spot the next down cycle and get out of their investment.

This development could be exacerbated by political pressure to regulate Bitcoin harder and, in some cases, downright ban it. Some countries will take the route of China, which in 2021 banned all cryptocurrency trading. This was due to concern over financial instability. At the same time, China is developing its own cryptocurrency tailored to the state's needs. Other countries are similarly already working on virtual versions of their fiat currencies. Introducing virtual fiat currencies could be the impetus for a more brutal crackdown on the less governable decentralized cryptocurrencies.

Cryptocurrencies would almost wholly be traded through offshore destinations outside the regulation of Western and Asian nation-states. Some territories and smaller sovereign countries will see an opportunity to provide the legal and financial framework for the cryptocurrency industry. This development is already underway with many cryptocurrency exchanges and companies established in the Caribbean and other jurisdictions outside US, Chinese, and European regulation.

If government fiat currencies were to adopt many of the features of cryptocurrencies with their local adaptions, the push to adopt bitcoin for regular people who are not necessarily against the government would be much smaller. On the other hand, if governments were to go from tolerating cryptocurrencies as is the case now to a more active antagonistic stance that would also pressure citizens with the threat of legal action, as is the case in China, it would significantly reduce the number of active users. This could result in a situation where the demand for bitcoin is reduced leading to a downward trend in the price. That would lead to a sell-off but not a complete abandonment since the true believers of Bitcoin, Bitcoin maximalists, and other people for whom the global and anonymous features of Bitcoin would continue to be helpful would continue to use it.

This scenario leads to different economics for the miners since the basis for their profitability is the value of bitcoin. Earlier we saw that bitcoin is tough to kill off completely since it will easily adapt to even massive drops in mining power. That would also happen in this scenario. Like any downward movement in bitcoin, the miners with the highest cost base for mining would be the first to see their profitability shrink and eventually disappear. This sets in motion a process whereby miners leave the network. While the total hash rate would drop, the difficulty of mining would adapt, which would decrease the cost of mining bitcoin, making it profitable for the remaining miners.

In this scenario then, bitcoin and cryptocurrencies would consolidate around a smaller user base than currently. It would consist of firm believers and people who need bitcoin for practical reasons. That could be cyber and other criminals, terrorists or freedom fighters (depending on how you look at their cause), and dissidents of oppressive regimes. Nevertheless, Bitcoin would still be the currency of choice to power black markets where absolute privacy is necessary. It could thus continue as a fringe virtual currency but with a significant scale.

Disappearance of the Nation-State

The previous two centuries have seen the rise of the modern nation-state as the primary mode of organization of people on the earth. Today, with very few exceptions, such as Antarctica, all land is in one way or another related to a nation-state. The highest global governance body is the United Nations. It has become so self-evident that we rarely pause to think that it is a recent anomaly in human civilization. Let us, therefore, reflect on other alternative modes of organization that have historically prevailed through larger periods of time.

The most foundational and ubiquitous is the tribe consisting of a band of people often closely related by kinship. Indeed kinship was the primary focus of anthropology when it emerged as a discipline to study human culture. Tribes continue to exist formally and informally within and across nation-states but are rarely endowed with sovereignty.

Historically, there is another mode of organization that has been dominant: the city-state. It is hard to think that well-known European nations such as Italy and Germany were emphatically not nation-states until little more than a hundred years ago but were dominated by local city-states for millennia. A city-state is similar to a nation-state but is defined by the extent of one city and its surrounding land. It is sovereign and self-contained. It does not depend on any outside entities. We know famous city-states like Venice, Athens, Rome, Babylon, and Bangkok. They still exist today even as sovereign entities like Monaco, Singapore, and Vatican City.

Another mode that has historically also held sway over large swathes of land for long periods of time is the empire or kingdom. These would often comprise city-states and territories belonging to tribes. Some empires have lasted for centuries but tend to be more volatile, and their extent changes continually, unlike the city-state. The empire usually depends on centralized governance with varying degrees of regional autonomy.

The premise of this scenario is that something happens that triggers the decline or fall of the modern nation-state as we know it. That could be due to losing relevance, new political developments, or violent upheaval like World War III. It would, therefore, probably revert to one of the other stable modes of human organization we have seen throughout history, that is, tribes, city-states, or empires.

A World War III could erupt in which the most significant nation-states decided to consolidate territory they felt they could claim, perhaps due to historical arguments or pure opportunism, which we see today in actions and rhetoric from Russia and China. That would see the emergence of a few large regional empires. However, it could also happen that smaller nation-states willfully gave up their sovereignty to seek the protection of a competing empire.

In this situation, much of the international banking system will be impaired. Empires would seek to establish their trading systems to exercise power over trade. That would leave the area of global trade open for competition since no globally accepted payment system like Swift would exist any longer. In such a situation, bitcoin would be very convenient for international payments and exchange since it is neutral. The fact that it is a currency truly ungovernable and not subject to the whims of any single entity (like the dollar is to American interests) allows it to emerge as a consensus payment system that will power cross-border payments.

A variant of this is that the nation-state peacefully starts to lose its significance and gives way to the city-state as the primary unit of organization of society. Some indication of how that process could unfold can already be seen in the United States where charter cities provide an example. The trend of increasing local governance would strengthen the development toward a situation where cities undertake most if not all of the needs of their people. The nation-state may still provide minimal services like defense and judicial systems. In this model, cities would be free to develop their own alternative currencies and payment solutions. Moving funds between these and supporting trade would necessitate an independent currency.

Cities could have local virtual currencies and blockchains to document official registries like deeds. The local currencies are used for rewards and can be used for paying city taxes. Since currency in this model would splinter into multiple local currencies, bitcoin would act as a reference currency. This would see the rise of the bitcoin standard against which currencies are pegged. Most trade would be done in the local currencies, but exchange between them would be done through bitcoin.

The last possibility is the rise of tribes as the primary mode of organization, which could happen inside the current nation-states and is to some extent already happening online. In China, Taobao villages provide the blueprint of such an online tribe. We also see that people increasingly find social groups online irrespective of physical proximity. In this model, the physical location, perhaps still dominated by the state, has lost its significance. This situation is similar to the state of affairs for tribes living on the fringe of empires or kingdoms for millennia.

As we saw earlier, the nation-state is the primary reason for the dominance of fiat currencies and the banking system. There are several different variants of how the nation-state could disappear or lose its prominence, which has tremendous consequences for exchange. In current society, we see indications of all of them, but we are still determining if these trends will continue or reverse. The historical developments leading to this differ, but interestingly, bitcoin assumes a prominent role in all variants of this scenario. Since Bitcoin is well-designed for fragmented transactionalism, it is well-suited for the fragmentation of the nation-state. It will increase its utility, not so much as a medium of exchange, but as a store of value primarily used for currency exchange.

The Singularity

The singularity is a shorthand for radical changes in humans' interaction with technology. It is a term originally coined by futurist and inventor Ray Kurzweil and, in mathematics, denotes a point where a function is undefined. The critical concept is exponential development, exemplified by Moore's law. The assumption is that ultimately, technological development will allow humans to upload their minds to a virtual world of software running on digital computer hardware. Our minds will be copied one-to-one to a software representation of our consciousness.

This is a possibility that philosophers such as David Chalmers, Max Tegmark, and Nick Bostrom have taken up. The technology for this has yet to arrive, but betting on the exponential improvement of technology, they assume that it will happen in the not-too-distant future. In this scenario, humans are thus finally able to partially or wholly live in virtual realities where the physical body is no longer present as the primary locus of experience and interaction.

Until now the economics of the singularity have not been widely analyzed though. It seems far-fetched that computers would run these virtual worlds of the uploaded transhuman experience just because they could. Even with a continuation of the exponential development of technology, it will not be free. No theoretical argument has been made that the singularity will produce technology without energy or maintenance. There will still be a physical world where energy needs to be created and hardware and software for the computers made and maintained.

It is reasonable to assume that uploaded humans would have to pay for their uploaded home somehow. Without a physical presence, that would have to be in a virtual currency. We can therefore imagine that uploaded humans will have to pay rent to the maintainers of their virtual worlds. Since eternal life in the metaverse can't be paid for with finite sums, the virtual avatars would need to work to pay the rent. Therefore, they will work and be paid in a virtual currency, which could very well be bitcoin. Alternatively, their savings could be in bitcoin, and the virtual world would have its own cryptocurrency that could be exchanged with bitcoin. What other features one could want to buy or trade in such a virtual world are only limited by imagination. It could be vacation in particularly interesting worlds that are lifelike copies of *The Lord of the Rings* or *Guardians of the Galaxy*, VIP zones in the company of famous people, or the opportunity for a next-generation ChatGPT-infused conversation with historical figures.

Similarly, the forms of work a virtual avatar could perform are interesting to think about. Web worker and virtual assistant are obvious candidates. Penetration tester, dark web private investigator, and researcher are other exciting options. The singularity sounds promising but would still require a currency to work.

Since the singularity to a large extent is a virtual existence, it seems fair to assume that virtual currencies would play a significant role. Since bitcoin is already the biggest, it would stand an excellent chance to be a significant currency or even the reserve currency of the metaverse.

Post-apocalypse

On a darker note, the entire human civilization as we know it with global commerce and communication could collapse. In this scenario, the world experiences a cataclysm with global implications. It could be a meteor impact, volcanic eruption, alien attack, or thermonuclear war. There are plenty of doomsday visions to choose from, but in this scenario, it would lead to global population collapse and a collapse of the global economy as we know it. There would be no more long-range travel and commerce. High-tech industry would disappear.

Humans would live in small bands or tribes as in the time of hunter-gatherers, perhaps underground. People would survive by farming and hunting, superficially resembling the hunter-gatherer days of the deep prehistoric past, but technology would not be gone. Much scavenged technology could be used, and know-how would still be preserved to some extent. Pre-apocalypse technology would become a scarce resource and be increasingly difficult to repair. Some new technology could perhaps be produced but would be at a much lower level and probably not digital since the production of semiconductors requires a pretty sophisticated ecosystem.

Ownership of computer hardware would be increasingly rare with time. Since virtual currencies depend on software running on computer chips, they would not be widespread since the utility of a medium of exchange that requires computers, which are not common, is low. Without an Internet, global currencies would not be feasible. Proof-of-work-based cryptocurrencies would not be viable since energy production would depend on technology and be scarce.

Consequently, in this scenario, Bitcoin disappears. Some blockchains might persist locally, if the apocalypse allows the production of some technology and energy. These could feature local networks where exchange could occur in virtual currencies, which could be blockchains but probably not proof-of-work-based ones. An apocalypse would mean the end of Bitcoin.

Interplanetary

In contemporary society, we see a new kind of drive toward space. Billionaires and nation-states have renewed humanity's interest in space exploration. The most immediate focus is on the moon and Mars whereto several missions are already planned. Moreover, rocket technology is improving radically for the first time since the space race of the 1960s, and new thinking abounds. This bodes well for an interplanetary future for humanity.

On the moon, vast cities could easily be constructed in underground lunar lava tubes. Since the moon has no atmosphere, it would become a convenient transport hub for interplanetary supply chains. The moon becomes the warehouse and distribution center of the solar system.

Building flexible space elevators would secure easy exchange of goods between Earth and the moon, such that all import and export with Earth does not rely on rockets. Unfortunately, even though the cost of rocket launches is decreasing, it will remain prohibitively expensive for interplanetary logistics to develop at scale.

The moon and Mars are not necessarily the only or best places for colonization. For example, Venus's higher atmosphere offers air density and pressure suitable for balloons. In fact it is the place most similar to

Earth in the entire solar system. Since it hosts large amounts of noble gases, it could be filled with high-altitude flying gas mining cities. In addition, the extraordinarily high concentration of CO_2 makes it easy to grow plants. For example, bioengineered airborne algae could gradually convert the atmosphere and reverse the runaway greenhouse effect by substituting CO_2 for oxygen. Eventually, air could even become breathable.

The moons of the big planets, such as Jupiter and Saturn, are currently the focus of many new exploratory space missions. Jupiter's moons contain large amounts of organic compounds, water, CO_2, and ammonia ice, which are conducive to supporting biological life. In this system, helium 3 and hydrogen could be harvested. Likewise, the Jovian system would become a waystation for colonizing the Cronian system of moons around Saturn. There are around 150 of these with a great variety of sizes and resources.

Humans could thus become a genuinely interplanetary species, permanently settling in several of the solar system's planets and moons. Like all colonization, trade is what fuels it, and this is no different. Interplanetary trade, though, requires a different kind of monetary system. The distance between them alone poses challenges. The light takes one hour and 20 minutes to reach Saturn from Earth. That means we will have to rethink the concept of time since current models are based on UTC, which is the time defined by the Greenwich Observatory near London on Earth. The general theory of relativity also predicts that time will "drift" between locations because of the different effects of gravity affecting time. Close to a large body like Jupiter, time will be different from a small one like the moon. Since Bitcoin depends critically on timestamps, this creates challenges that have to be resolved.

A new interplanetary standard will therefore need to be developed. It could define time from the lighthouse effect of known pulsars. Pulsars are rapidly rotating magnetic neutron stars. The rotation frequency is stable, thereby offering a way to determine time, independent of Earth or the physical properties of atomic watches affected by gravity. This new timestamp could become the new basis for interplanetary trade.

Communication will be done through lasers to establish an interplanetary Internet. Transactions will now take longer to clear. Local currencies will dominate different parts of the solar system, but Bitcoin or a modified version could theoretically become the interstellar reserve currency used for interplanetary trade. Still, it is difficult to see how miners in different regions of space with up to an hour and a half can run a shared bitcoin network and blockchain where solutions for the next block are found every ten minutes. If a miner on Titan finds a solution, how will that be accepted by the entire network when it takes an hour and a half to reach every miner? How do you prevent double spending across so significant time differences? Transactions of the same balance could be made in several different "time zones." Bitcoin is conceptualized as an Earth-based currency and will not work as is as an interplanetary one.

Will There Be Bitcoin in the Future?

We have now considered six different scenarios that change assumptions of society, technology, and politics to understand how Bitcoin could develop. The first variable concerns change in human society ranging from none in the two first scenarios to radical change in the last two. Along with this, we considered the parameter of technological change ranging from none to decline to radical. The last parameter was government control. This parameter concerns the degree to which central governments and supra-national structures are able to control the development and use of Bitcoin—these range from a high degree of control to none.

Table 11-1. *Bitcoin under different future scenarios*

Scenario	Societal Change	Technological Change	Government Control	Bitcoin
Normalization	No change	No change	Increased positive	Becomes mainstream, increased usage
Fringe consolidation	No change	No change	Increased negative	Focused on the "dark" economy, decreased usage
Disappearance of nation-states	Substantial	No change	Decreased	The Bitcoin standard, increased usage
Singularity	Substantial	Radical	Disappeared	Becomes reserve currency, increased usage
Post-apocalypse	Radical	Decline	Disappeared	Disappears
Interplanetary	Radical	Radical	Decreased	Disappears

Under all scenarios except those involving radical societal change, Bitcoin will survive, and in most of them, it will probably thrive. For the Bitcoin standard to emerge, nation-states must disappear as the primary locus of political control. To become mainstream, Bitcoin has to change, or at least how it is used. The more speculative scenarios are more challenging for Bitcoin. The singularity is compatible with Bitcoin as the reserve currency of choice. Still, in a post-apocalyptic world, the lack of reliable production and maintenance of hardware and energy undermines the feasibility of Bitcoin. It seems structurally poised for a future as an interplanetary reserve currency, but unfortunately, physics gets in the way of establishing an interplanetary Bitcoin mining network.

We may conclude that Bitcoin seems likely to prosper in the future if society doesn't change radically but also that it may be obsolete if it does. These are just possible scenarios from which one can infer one's subjective probability. The fact that most are favorable to Bitcoin is thus not necessary if the most likely one is the unfavorable scenario. I will let it be up to the reader to make their assessments.

CHAPTER 12

Beyond

We saw in the introduction how, in his book *Hyperobjects*, Timothy Morton describes a type of objects of such grand temporal and spatial proportions that they defy regular ideas about what a thing is. He mentions several examples of hyperobjects, such as an oil spill, climate change, the solar system, and radioactive material. Unfortunately, contradictions proliferate in his characterization of hyperobjects, making it hard to follow and draw any general conclusions that can be used for further investigations.

Still, there is one important key idea worth noting in the context of Bitcoin. Morton builds on a contemporary philosophical movement called object-oriented ontology, which derives its metaphysics from Heidegger, who holds that the world cannot be adequately understood by privileging human existence. Object-oriented ontology postulates that objects also exist beyond human perception, which can only be grasped obliquely, if at all.

Hyperobjects, as they appear from the characterization of Morton, bring to mind an inert mechanistic reactive existence subject merely to cause and effect. Although they exist in a complex multidimensional or "hyper world" that is hard to grasp, they are still just objects. But a thing like Bitcoin is not simply an object in this sense, even if it is hyper. It does more than merely react to events in the world; it also acts by itself on the world. Whereas objects react to manipulations from their environment, only organisms act on the environment in a way that simple dynamics cannot describe. This is a crucial insight that points to the possibility that

© Anders Lisdorf 2023
A. Lisdorf, *Still Searching for Satoshi*, https://doi.org/10.1007/978-1-4842-9639-4_12

we may speak of hyperorganisms in the same sense as Morton speaks of hyperobjects, that is, as entities outside the immediate perception of humans that we can know only obliquely.

Hyperorganisms would be challenging to detect, like hyperobjects are, because they act on different scales than the human scale. By human scale, I mean the scale easily perceived by humans in terms of time and space. Hyperorganisms may not be bound to the same limited locality a human inhabits nor the same timeframe. They may not move fast enough for us to perceive or even move at all in the traditional sense. Their actions could have a hidden logic, but we cannot be sure to comprehend it. A hyperorganism would be to humans what a human is to bacteria. The human body is perceptible for bacteria and an integral part of their environment. But the bacteria would only be aware of a tiny sliver of the entire organism and would not ever question whether their environment is part of a higher-order system. Suppose bacteria developed the ability to communicate as humans do. In that case, they may start to comprehend more aspects of the totality of the organism by integrating knowledge from other bacteria in different areas of the body. With ingenuity and imagination, they may even develop a good understanding of the logic of this type of entity called human.

The characterization of a hyperorganism is similar to the parable of the blind men and the elephant that can be traced back to some of the earliest Buddhist texts, such as the Tittha Sutta from around 500 BCE. The parable describes how the blind men in a village go to inspect an elephant. One touched its trunk and concluded it was like a snake, another its ear and figured it was like a fan, while a third felt its leg and figured it was like a pillar. All came up with vastly different conceptions of what an elephant is, much like the different bacteria would of a human. The challenge we will take up here is similar. We will integrate the diverse knowledge about Bitcoin that we have gained in the course of this book. Each chapter may provide clues to the enigmatic nature of the hyperentity that is Bitcoin.

Giving up the human perspective is a powerful tool to open our minds to the possibility of hyperorganisms whose existence transcends human perception. Therefore, we need to build a new theoretical framework, without which we would be unable to see them.

Is There Life Out There?

Today there is already a search for life beyond humans taking place. NASA and others in the field of astrobiology search for extraterrestrial life. This is done by looking into space according to assumptions about what life is. Unfortunately, the result is that the criteria by which we search for extraterrestrial life are almost identical to known life forms. We take the human or at least terrestrial perspective when we define criteria for finding life outside of Earth. We, therefore, need to step back and reflect a bit more on what life is.

What Is Life?

We are alive, as are the plants, animals, and fungi around us. They show vast differences in appearance and character. Think of the microbes living in the depths of the Kidd Mine 350 miles northwest of Toronto undisturbed for up to two billion years in total darkness who don't need oxygen and live of fools' gold. The Deep Carbon Observatory, a research project studying life inside the earth, estimates that the total biomass of these organisms is 300 times as much as all living humans.

Another example is the fungus *Ophiocordyceps*, which causes the carpenter ants to climb to a high point of vegetation, grip it, and die. The fungus will then grow its fruiting bodies from the body of the insect to propagate.

A final example of the immense diversity of life is lichen, which grows as a cover on stone and wood. Lichen is not in fact one species but a composite symbiotic species consisting of algae or cyanobacteria and different species of fungi. The species of lichen called *Rhizocarpon geographicum* is estimated to be able to become more than 8,000 years old, making it the oldest living organism. This species is estimated to cover 6–8% of the earth's land surface.

Life is stranger and more multifaceted than most can imagine. Still, there is no doubt in our minds that they all share this quality called life. Even if this is self-evident, it is challenging to say precisely what life is. Some researchers have nevertheless tried to pinpoint what the essence of life is.

The Austrian physicist Erwin Schrödinger provided one of the first philosophical answers to this question from the perspective of physics. In his book *What Is Life?* he found that the characteristic feature of life is that an entity "(...) goes on 'doing something,' moving exchanging material with its environment." By doing this, it avoids the fate inscribed in all things in the universe, that of being destroyed by entropy. Entropy can be thought of as the degree of disorder in a closed system. The second law of thermodynamics states that with time the entropy or disorder of a closed system increases. Schrödinger noted that any nonliving entity quickly reaches the state of thermodynamic equilibrium or "maximum entropy." Living beings, however, do not rapidly reach this state but continue to be ordered.

The explanation for this, according to Schrödinger, is that the organism eats, drinks, and breathes; more precisely, they have a metabolism by which they exchange something with the environment. Traditionally metabolism has been viewed as one of matter or energy, but that does not make sense according to Schrödinger; instead, he proposed the surprising solution that living organisms draw negative entropy from their environment. In this view, "(...) the device by which an organism maintains itself at a fairly high level of orderliness (= low level of entropy) really consists in continually sucking orderliness from its environment (...) in the case of higher animals we know the kind of orderliness they feed upon (...) the extremely well-ordered state of matter in more or less complicated organic compounds, which serve them as foodstuffs. After utilizing it, they return it in a very much degraded form." According to Schrödinger then, life is a process by which, through metabolism, order is maintained by taking it from the environment.

The Chilean biologist Humberto Maturana had for years been teaching biology to his students and came up short with the simplest of questions, namely, what life is. He was unable to find convincing answers in previous work in biology. This provoked years of thinking about the essential nature of living systems. To answer the question, he had to invent a new term, *autopoiesis*: "An autopoietic machine is a machine organized (defined as a unity) as a network of processes of production (transformation and destruction) of components which: (i) through their interactions and transformations continuously regenerate and realize the network of processes (relations) that produced them; and (ii) constitute it (the machine) as a concrete unity in space in which they (the components) exist by specifying the topological domain of its realization as such a network."

Like the entire book *Autopoiesis and Cognition: The Realization of the Living*, the quote is very concise and difficult to unwrap. The main point is that a living system is autopoietic, and an autopoietic system is able to regenerate its own constitution continuously. We, humans, are able to continue to regenerate our bodies by finding the food and nutrients we need by ourselves. The same is the case for plants and animals. This contrasts with an allopoietic system, like a factory, which also uses raw materials but produces something other than itself. Autopoiesis can thus be described as the ability to continuously create the conditions for the system's continued existence. That is the essence of life, according to Maturana.

A living system is characterized by the ability to sustain its own constitution over a prolonged period through metabolism with the environment. All known examples are biological, but the principles we have reviewed here do not require biological chemical compounds. A living system could exist that matched the criteria for life but was not based on known biochemical processes. A hyperorganism might fulfill all the same criteria, but if we found such a hyperorganism, how would we determine if it were alive?

We might define and characterize it in much the same way as biological life. Even if we are not looking for the exact biological mechanisms that we know of for terrestrial life, we should look for the same characteristics that we find in biological life.

Characteristics of Life and Bitcoin

In biology there is no unanimously agreed-upon definition of the characteristics of life, but it is common to require an organized structure that can reproduce and metabolize, react to stimuli, grow, and adapt.

Structure

All living systems have a structure defined by a boundary delineating what is inside and outside. For example, the cell has a cell membrane, while animals have skin. For Bitcoin, we have a different type of structure. Each instance of the Bitcoin code runs on a CPU that it shares with other programs. The structure, in this sense, is the processes initiated by the Bitcoin code. But Bitcoin is defined by another more important structure as a hyperorganism, that of the Bitcoin network. All instances running on the Bitcoin blockchain and connected to other nodes define the boundary of Bitcoin. Nodes running a Bitcoin code not connected to others are not part of the structure of Bitcoin. The same is the case if they are using a different blockchain. The structure of Bitcoin as a hyperorganism is, therefore, different from currently known biological species. It resembles fungal hyphae, though. A fungus grows as a network of hyphae, which are thin tubular threads through the environment. Its structure is thus defined by the hyphae connected to it. Similarly, all nodes connected to the Bitcoin network define the organism of Bitcoin.

Reproduction

For an organism to reproduce, there must be heredity. For living systems on the earth, this is achieved through DNA. In common parlance, it is called the gene, which contains all the necessary instructions to produce the organism. The author of the groundbreaking book *The Selfish Gene*, Richard Dawkins, argues that the gene is interesting in its role as a replicator. It uses bodies, which he calls survival machines, in order to get reproduced. Darwinian selection makes sure that only the genes that are best at making this happen will survive in the long run. The distinction between the replicator and the vessel doing the replication is crucial. In biology, the replicator is the gene and the vessel the body. But Dawkins argues for a universal Darwinism where these laws apply everywhere. We should therefore be able to look at something similar for hyperorganisms.

For Bitcoin, the replicator is the source code since this describes all the components to build Bitcoin. The leap from DNA code to computer code is not particularly big. The main difference is that computer code is base 2 implemented in semi-conductors, where only one and zero exist. DNA is base 4 implemented in organic chemistry since there are four possible values, those of the four different nucleotides: cytosine (C), guanine (G), adenine (A), and thymine (T). We will return to the vessel for replication shortly.

Adaptation

Adaptation is an organism's ability to change its gene to survive if living conditions change. Historically, mutations have provided change that ensured adaptation through the process of natural selection, but humans have also done this through selective breeding of cultivated species, genetically modified crops, and gene therapy. For Bitcoin, adaptation is achieved through the open source developers' continuous maintenance of its source code, designed to adapt it to the Bitcoin ecosystem's changing conditions. With each new code release, new problems encountered in the environment are addressed to make Bitcoin better adapted. This, in turn, creates a new environment with new pressures. The current code of Bitcoin is heavily edited and expanded compared with the original, which shows that adaptation has already occurred. Following Richard Dawkins's influential theory of the selfish gene, adaptability works at the phenotypical level, that is, the organism that the gene produces, but that is not always the whole story. The gene gives rise to what Dawkins calls the extended phenotype. This concept encapsulates both the biological organism the gene codes for directly and any effects on other organisms or the environment the gene promotes. The most impressive example from the animal kingdom is the beaver, which builds dams to change the environment to favor its survival. The extended phenotype of Bitcoin is the Bitcoin network, the open source developers, and all the Bitcoin enthusiasts. This extended phenotype, rather than the software running the Bitcoin code, is the unit of adaptation. While the code is the replicator, in Dawkins's terms, this extended phenotype is the vessel.

Metabolism

Biological life metabolizes chemical compounds and energy through an interaction with its environment. A cell takes substances from the environment and uses them for chemical reactions. This requires energy.

Plants use the sun's energy to create organic material that animals can metabolize. All living systems take something from the environment, metabolizing it into waste. This waste may be crucial for other organisms. A system of organisms tied together in this way is an ecosystem. In a nonorganic sense, Bitcoin can also be said to metabolize. It takes electrical energy to power the CPU running its computer code, which it metabolizes to currency, which humans can use for monetary purposes. Money is, so to say, the waste product of Bitcoin but the key to the ecosystem of which it is a part. This ecosystem is the international world of finance. Bitcoin thus forms a symbiotic relationship with humans and resembles mycorrhizal fungi, which create large underground networks connecting to plant roots through which they exchange nutrients with the plants.

Growth

The power to grow is the ability of a living system to reconstitute its shape. No tissue can exist for the duration of a lifetime of an organism without degrading. For example, the heart beats around 3,600 times an hour or about 91,980,000 times in a lifetime. No material exists that can withstand that. The different parts of biological organisms are thus able to regenerate. Bitcoin has found a clever way to make it happen since it has coopted the human brain to motivate us to repeatedly install its program on multiple computers. This effect has been achieved through religious zeal, the promise of quick gains, and associations with a bright and more just future. Bitcoin has inserted itself into the behavioral agenda of humans. We buy and install Bitcoin because it comes with a promise of salvation or at least an easy buck. In this way, Bitcoin resembles the species of fungi known as *Ophiocordyceps* that has somehow been able to manipulate the behavior of insects as part of its extended phenotype. A bleak parody of this analysis would have us be like the zombies in the HBO show *The Last of Us*, affected by a new strain of cordyceps mindlessly going about doing the business of Bitcoin, which is to proliferate. This, of course, is a caricature, and the effects of Bitcoin on humans seem somewhat more benign, but the mechanism is essentially the same and well-known in the animal kingdom. Bitcoin grows through a careful orchestration of human motives and behavior. This is part of its extended phenotype.

Reaction to Stimuli

The ability to respond to environmental stimuli is important for any organism's survival. Animals do this, for example, when their bodies are depleted of nutrients by responding with hunger signals. This sets in motion behavior to replenish the needed nutrients. When too close to fire, we feel pain, which motivates us to move away from the fire. These are subsystems that have the purpose of maintaining the equilibrium of the body in a state conducive to continued existence. There is no immediately obvious analogy when we consider Bitcoin in this light. It does not move. But many biological organisms do not move either. There is, though, one way in which Bitcoin shows an ability to react to stimuli. This is through the setting of the difficulty of the cryptographic puzzle. Every time a new block is created, it looks at the time since the last block. If this is longer than ten minutes, it means that the total processing capacity of the Bitcoin network is low, and it reconfigures the difficulty to a lower level. Conversely, if the time is shorter, it means there is an excess of computing power relative to the equilibrium of ten minutes, and the difficulty is increased. This subtle heartbeat of the Bitcoin network makes sure that it adapts to the processing power available in its surroundings, that is, the computers it lives in.

Is Bitcoin Alive?

According to the criteria of life, we can conclude that Bitcoin seems to fulfill them. Even though Bitcoin does not rely on organic chemistry like all other known life forms, it appears to have the same properties. A counterargument could be that Bitcoin is not really alive since it depends on computers and the Internet. But that is no different than many bacteria that require very particular environments, without which they will die. Another possible criticism is that humans created it. But that is not an actual argument because there are no criteria that require life not to be created artificially. It also resembles life in the way that it recombines features from other sources. We saw how different strands of technological developments led to the implementation of Bitcoin. This is no different from how bacteria recombine and absorb genetic material from other bacteria. The process is well-known in biology.

Bitcoin, therefore, fulfills the essential functions of life as we defined it previously: "a living system can therefore be said to be characterized by the ability to sustain its own constitution over a prolonged period through metabolism with the environment." Bitcoin is also autopoietic in that it continuously coopts humans to install and upgrade the software that runs it. The Bitcoin miners running the Bitcoin network today are not the same as the ones ten years ago. It dynamically replaces the nodes that implement its code. It also has a metabolism by which it takes energy to power computer CPUs and metabolizes it to digital currency, which its symbiont, humans, can spend to buy more energy.

One might also counter that this is a fictional just-so story that can be told about anything that runs on a computer. Let us, therefore, consider whether that is true by considering a few other examples of computer-based systems. First, let us look at the computer worm. Like an actual virus, it only replicates and is not alive. It has no metabolism or adaptability. It is the same code.

Another example is a popular computer program like Microsoft Word. Humans also help reproduce it, and it has adapted through the continuous release of new versions, but it does not respond to stimuli and has no metabolism. A closer analogy to Bitcoin is perhaps a peer-to-peer sharing system like BitTorrent since it has a similar morphology to Bitcoin. It is installed on a computer and connects to other nodes. BitTorrent does bring value in the form of digital assets, but it does not produce these, so it cannot be said to have metabolism in the same sense as Bitcoin; it is merely a transport system for something else and, therefore, allopoietic. As can be seen, even close parallels are somewhat lacking to fulfill the criteria for life in the way that Bitcoin does.

Putting the Elephant Back Together

We are therefore left with the surprising conclusion that Bitcoin as a hyperorganism might, in fact, be alive. It will, of course, require more research and thinking than has been offered here to be verified. It is but a brief sketch. Still, this discovery provides fruitful avenues for further investigation: Are other similar hyperorganisms hiding in plain sight around us? What are the consequences of this? Precisely what kind of biological organisms does Bitcoin resemble? How did it become alive out of something that was not alive? Most of all, does the reasoning presented here hold up to further scrutiny? I hope that such questions can be answered in the future.

In this book, we have considered many different aspects of Bitcoin. When we consider Bitcoin as a hyperorganism, these different perspectives come together, like the different parts of the elephant examined by the blind men. Each observation by one of the blind men is similar to one or more of the chapters in this book. From its own perspective, it provides fascinating insights into one aspect of Bitcoin. One aspect is the technological history that explains the heritage of Bitcoin and, in biological terms, provides a phylogenetic account of how the species of Bitcoin came into existence. The history of Satoshi provides the precise historical context of how Bitcoin happened in the world or the ontogenetic account in biological terms. The investigation into the nature of money offers insight into how Bitcoin can produce its critical effect: monetary value. The social organization accounts for the social structures that help it grow as a part of its extended phenotype. The religious aspect explains the mechanism by which Bitcoin motivates us humans to provide continued support for its proliferation in a symbiotic relationship. The future perspectives provide ecological scenarios about the future destiny of Bitcoin as a hyperorganism.

If the blind men touching the elephant had not insisted that they each held the proper understanding of what this thing called an elephant was but instead had tried to communicate and bring together these isolated truths, they could have come close to understanding and conceptualizing this elephant. This was the secret plan of this book: to bring together different perspectives on Bitcoin that are each true in isolation but insufficient to understand Bitcoin. By integrating these perspectives, we are able to provide the foundation for a more comprehensive and extensive understanding of Bitcoin as a new type of entity, a hyperorganism.

APPENDIX

Possible Identities of Satoshi

In this appendix, we will look in more detail at the different persons that could have been the real person behind the pseudonym Satoshi Nakamoto. The selection is based on clues related to the writings of Satoshi. The first input of potential identities is derived from the references that are directly cited in the Bitcoin whitepaper. All people specifically mentioned as authors of papers cited are listed here. The second input is from the cypherpunk mailing list since the thinking and ideas for Bitcoin are clearly derived from there, specifically Wei Dai's B-money and Adam Back's Hashcash proposals. Since these two texts are foundational for Bitcoin, the historical person behind Satoshi would probably have engaged in conversations about these.

Only people with a real name and some independently verifiable information about them have been included here. Anonymous and pseudonymous contributors have not been included since we don't know who they are.

© Anders Lisdorf 2023
A. Lisdorf, *Still Searching for Satoshi*, https://doi.org/10.1007/978-1-4842-9639-4

Cited Authors in the Bitcoin Whitepaper

Wei Dai

Wei Dai is a Chinese-American computer scientist. He is a very private person, and the name is a relatively common Chinese name. It is, therefore, limited what we can say about him. According to his Wikipedia page, he graduated with a BS in computer science from the University of Washington. We don't know exactly, when but according to his website, he was active in the extropian community and the cryptography mailing list at the end of the 1990s. This would probably have coincided with his days as a student.

He developed the Crypto++ library in C++ in 1995, which is his earliest known work, and co-authored a publication with Josh Benaloh from the same year.

This fits well with an education starting in the mid-1990s, making Dai's probable date of birth fall within the span of 1970–1975. He is evidently proficient in C++, as we saw would be expected for someone educated then. So far, he would be a good fit for Satoshi, but he is not a native British English speaker. He writes in American English. While his B-money paper is quoted in the Bitcoin whitepaper, it served more as an idea that could shape the direction than as a concrete implementation guide. Specifically, there does not seem to be anything in Dai's publications or other writings indicating he has any in-depth knowledge about peer-to-peer communication or proof of work. Furthermore, he seems to keep publishing proficiently about entirely different subjects while Bitcoin was being developed, like decision theory, Vhash security, and hash collisions. Reading his posts on the various groups and mailing lists, he seems more philosophical and interested in fundamental issues of physics and the nature of the universe than a practical monetary activist. To put it another way, B-money was just one of his thoughtful philosophical ideas.

Dai has shared three emails that Satoshi wrote to him before the publication of the whitepaper, but they are much later, and emails are easy to tamper with. There is no evidence he has ever been to the United Kingdom or London, but then again there is very little evidence of anything related to his whereabouts. He seems to reside on the US west coast, which can be deduced from his company Bitvise's web page. Bitvise was founded by Wei Dai and Denis Bider. In web archive snapshots of the "About us" page from the period of 2008 to 2010, it is mentioned that one co-founder, Dennis Bider, is living in St. Kitts and Nevis and the other (Dai) in Seattle, Washington. That would put Dai in Seattle in the Pacific time zone, which we saw did not fit well with Satoshi's documented activity pattern.

While Dai does fit many of the parameters of the Satoshi profile, other pieces of evidence fit to a lesser degree. But his language alone makes it unlikely that he would be the person behind Satoshi. It is, therefore, unlikely that Dai is Satoshi.

The KU Leuven Group
Jean-Jacques Quisquater

The Belgian professor of cryptography Jean-Jacques Quisquater is the lead author of a paper on a timestamp server. He is known to have been the first to implement a blockchain. He was born in 1945 and educated in Université Paris-Sud and finished with a doctoral thesis in 1987. He was the leader of the UCL Crypto Group based in Katholieke Universiteit (KU) Leuven in Belgium.

From 2007 to 2009, the period when Satoshi worked intensely on Bitcoin, he authored or co-authored no less than 52 papers on an impressive array of subjects ranging from RFID, cryptanalysis, and authentication. Nothing in his immense publication list seems to be related to virtual currencies, proof of work, or peer-to-peer computing. While living in the identified time zone, he is not British or based in the

United Kingdom. He does not seem to be coding at all. Quisquater does not fit Satoshi's profile well. He is too old, and the language and skills do not fit. Only the time zone seems to be a really good fit.

Xavier Serret Avila

He was one of the collaborators of Quisquater in Leuven. He was also part of the UCL Crypto Group. He is Spanish and got his master's in computer science at the Universitát Politecnica de Catalunya between 1990 and 1995. His age profile, therefore, seems to fit. He lived in Belgium from 2004 to 2011, which puts him in the correct time zone. There is also evidence that he did indeed work with C++ as a security architect in Santa Clara between 1999 and 2001. His focus was on music copy protection, and he invented a mechanism that would allow music to be plaid only on existing devices and not copied to new ones.

He does not seem to be a native English speaker and has no demonstrated interest or skills related to virtual currencies, peer-to-peer computing, or proof of work. Although the age and programming language fit, Avilla does not appear to match the Satoshi profile.

Henri Massias

Like Avila, Henri Massias worked at the UCL Crypto Group in Leuven. There is not much information to be found about him. He is French-speaking. After the paper cited in the Bitcoin whitepaper, he co-authored the article on "timestamping" with Stuart Haber in 2005. After that, there are no publications until 2013, when he started to publish about microscopy. He is currently employed by the Université de Limoges. There is little information to be found about Massias, but what we can find provides a bad fit with the profile. While the age seems to be right to judge by pictures and earliest publications, being a French speaker does not. His documented publishing after 2005 is in the area of microscopy, indicating a shift away from cryptography. There is no evidence that he was ever interested in or working on virtual currencies, peer-to-peer computing, or proof of work or proficient in C++. It is, therefore, highly improbable that Massias is Satoshi.

The Blockchain Inventors
Stuart Haber

The American cryptographer Stuart Haber is known as the inventor of the idea of the blockchain together with Wakefield Scott Stornetta. He started his education at Harvard in 1974, earning a BA in mathematics. IN 1978–1979 he studied in Paris at the Ecole Normale Superieure, after which he returned to Stanford until 1982. He switched to Columbia where he got his PhD in 1987. His age therefore does not fit the profile of Satoshi. Furthermore, he writes in American English and lives in the United States. Haber is highly unlikely to be Satoshi.

Wakefield Scott Stornetta

Haber's collaborator, Wakefield Scott Stornetta, is an American physicist who was born in 1959. He got his bachelor's in physics from Brigham Young University in 1983 and his PhD from Stanford in 1989. While he is a self-professed libertarian, he has no proven skills in peer-to-peer systems, programming, or virtual currencies. He writes American English and lives in the United Staes. It is, therefore, implausible he is Satoshi.

David Allen Bayer

The American mathematician David Allen Bayer was born 1955 and studied as an undergraduate at Swarthmore College. He earned his PhD in 1982. He authored a paper with Stornetta and Haber, where they incorporated Merkle trees in the blockchain, something Satoshi used in Bitcoin. Apart from that, there is nothing that fits the profile of Satoshi.

Bayer is older, writes American English, and lives in the United States, and there is no evidence he knows how to program. Bayer is, therefore, also highly unlikely to be Satoshi.

The Odd Men Out
Ralph C. Merkle

The renowned computer scientist and mathematician Ralph Merkle played an outsized role, as we saw, in the development of the foundational technologies for Bitcoin, such as hashing and public key cryptography. He was born in 1952 and educated in Berkeley in the 1970s. He writes in American English and has no known skills in C++, peer-to-peer computing, or virtual currencies. Since 2006 he has been based on the west coast. He, therefore, does not fit the profile of Satoshi.

William Feller

The American mathematician William Feller is easy to dismiss as a potential match. He was born in 1906 and died in 1970, well before C++ was even invented. It is impossible that he is Satoshi.

The Last Man Standing

So far, we had no luck finding even one candidate among the cited people that was even a possible fit for the profile of Satoshi. The lone remaining candidate is Adam Back, the author of Hashcash. Let us see how he compares to the Satoshi profile. The first thing worthy of notice is that he is the first British person on the list. He was born in 1970 and got his PhD in computer science from the University of Exeter in 1995. The PhD was on peer-to-peer computing, and the code for the thesis was written in C++. After graduation he has worked as a consultant according to his LinkedIn page.

Back's English is decidedly British and flawless. He was part of the cypherpunk mailing list and was particularly interested in virtual currencies. This can be seen from the fact that he was one of the few who responded excitedly to Wei Dai's post about B-money.

He published several articles in academic journals. His 2001 "Traffic Analysis Attacks and Trade-Offs in Anonymity Providing Systems" is co-authored with Ulf Möller and Anton Stiglic and published in the *Journal of Information Hiding*, which uses a citation style identical to the one used in the Bitcoin whitepaper. The author instructions for the journal can be seen to match the Bitcoin whitepaper (`www.techscience.com/jihpp/info/auth_instru`)

In a snapshot from 2009 of his website, cypherspace, he mentions his mother-in-law's Burmese cats page, from which we can deduce that he was married at the time Satoshi was writing. And he was living in London. Here we can also see that at the time Satoshi joined the P2P Foundation list, Back was also a member of the P2P hacker list at `https://web.archive.org/web/20081217163356/http://www.cypherspace.org/adam/`.

Only crypto and cypherpunk lists were listed apart from this. He also has a distributed systems section with publications with his supervisor Stephen Turner.

Back was thus British speaking, born in the 1970s, married, and living in London. He had the highest degree from a university, a PhD, and has a proven publishing record with the same citation style as the Bitcoin whitepaper. He is proficient in C++ and is not only familiar with but the author of the proof-of-work part of Bitcoin. He is also a specialist in P2P computing and has an avid interest in virtual currencies and cryptography. In short, we have evidence that Adam Back matches every single aspect of the profile for Satoshi.

Cryptography Mailing List

Now let us turn to the people on the cypherpunk mailing list. The following contains a list of all identifiable people responding to Dai's B-money post and Back's Hashcash post.

Anil Dash

He made very little imprint on the Internet. He has 13 posts on the cypherpunk-mailing list. I can find a few reviews by him on cryptography books. His email is from Silicon Graphics. He might have been a tech writer for a while (www.techcircle.in/author/anil-das). But it is almost impossible to say if it is the same person since this is a relatively common name.

Paul E. Foley

He was on cypherpunks from 1996 to 1997. The post was his penultimate post. His email address seems to be from a New Zealand broadband provider (https://mailing-list-archive.cryptoanarchy.wiki/authors/paul_foley_mycroft_at_actrix_gen_nz).

Again, his name is a fairly common name with many potential hits. It is consequently difficult to find the correct one, but since he is probably based in New Zealand, he is not a god fit.

Paul Bradley

He was fairly active with more than 200 posts from 1996 to 1998. He uses an email address from a UK broadband Internet provider, demons.co.uk. His web page is about cryptography (www.fatmans.demon.co.uk/). In 1997, it showed the web page of the company Datacom Technologies, which seems to have built websites (https://web.archive.org/web/19961227004711/http://www.fatmans.demon.co.uk/). It was "situated in the Hastings area of East Sussex." It links to Adam Back's homepage among many others (www.fatmans.demon.co.uk/crypt/links.htm).

He does not work in C++, though. On his page he writes: "I can provide design and consultancy services in HTML, CGI, Java, Animated GIFs, Real Audio, SSL and other security and encryption products." He is a Java programmer then and not a good fit.

Kent Crispin

Kent Crispin was very active with almost 300 posts. He was offering web development at his website www.songbird.com (https://web.archive.org/web/19970413233538/http://songbird.com/) and also offered consulting and hosting web pages. On his LinkedIn page (www.linkedin.com/in/kent-crispin-a783357/), it can be seen that he is based in California but retired now. He went to Caltech from 1972 to 1980 and Stanford at a later point. That means he doesn't match the location, nationality, and age of the profile of Satoshi.

Steve Schear

With 166 documented posts on the cypherpunk mailing list, Steve Schear was fairly active. His listed email address is from netcom.com, which provides Internet access and web hosting. The company is based in the United States. This could be his Twitter profile, https://twitter.com/p01ndexter, since it links to the Wikipedia page for cypherpunks. I also found a probable LinkedIn page for him, www.linkedin.com/in/stevenschear/, where he lists himself as a cypherpunk since 1994. It also locates him in the United States.

He seems to have been working at Tetherless, a mesh wireless system, around the time of his posts. Schear worked on a digital cash project, eCache, which was a digital gold provider from 2007 to 2014. He thus effectively ran a competitor to Bitcoin. His first job was in 1986, so he is too old to fit the age of the profile.

Robert Costner

Robert Costner has an email from efga.org, which in 1997 was Electronic Frontiers Georgia (today the domain is owned by EFGA Containers). The email address seems to be the administrator of the site as it is mentioned as the one to mail to on the website. Costner is consequently based in Georgia and seems primarily interested in online freedom, not virtual currencies. The EFGA is a nonprofit organization as can be seen from the Wikipedia page. Costner who was a computer store owner was a cofounder of the organization in 1995 where it was set up as a response to the Georgia House Bill 1630 (HB1630) that attempted to ban anonymous speech on the Internet. Beyond activism for digital rights in the late 1990s, no other evidence was found for Robert Costner.

Joe Randall Farmer

The email address is from hiwaay.net, an Internet provider based in the United States. There is no information about Joe Randall Farmer apart from the posts.

Timothy C. May

Timothy May is the infamous American founder of the crypto-anarchy movement that spawned the cypherpunk mailing list that was the predecessor of the cryptography mailing list. He was born 1951 and was based on the US west coast. There is no evidence that he could code in C++

and does not fit the profile. Even if he did, it would be hard to imagine him having time given his impressive activity on the cypherpunk mailing list and other places.

William H. Geiger III

There are many people by the name William Geiger III, and it is not possible to pinpoint precisely which one is the right one. He seems to have been involved with OpenPGP since he has an OpenPGP email address and made a version of PGP (PGP2.63-sha1). It was coded in Java (since it is a JAR file), so while he was able to code cryptographic systems, it was not in C++.

Robert Hettinga

Robert Hettinga is a well-known technical and political writer. His publications are numerous and go back to 1970. His website, http:// shipwright.com, seems to be very old and does not seem to be updated since 1998 but is still active. It indicates he is based in Boston and mentions the Digital Commerce Society of Boston, which is also mentioned on a LinkedIn page with the name Robert Hettinga (www.linkedin.com/in/ roberthettinga/?originalSubdomain=ai). That profile indicates he studied for a BA in philosophy at the University of Missouri-Columbia. There is no indication that he was coding anything.

Michael Johnson

Only 25 posts exist from Michael Johnson, and the email domain of the website is mejl.com, which is not currently active. He has a website with his own name (https://mljohnson.org). Here we can see that he was in the Army until 1984. He was an electrical engineer for 16 years, and in 2000 he went into being a full-time Christian missionary. He links to a contact form at this site: `https://cryptography.org/mpj/`. He also seems to have created encryption algorithms in 1995 and a ZIP algorithm in 1996 according to Bruce Schneier's website (`www.schneier.com/books/applied-cryptography-source/`). Johnson has a BA in electrical engineering and later an MA in electrical engineering. His age and time in the Army do not fit the profile of Satoshi well.

Gé Weijers

I found him on LinkedIn (`www.linkedin.com/in/gé-weijers-75b1b65/`). He worked at Progressive Systems in 1996, which is where his email listed on the cryptography mailing list is from. This shows he is Dutch and studied in Holland in 1981–1986 and puts him in the United States from 1996 until today. Now he is in the Arizona and Nevada area, close to Pacific Time. He therefore does not fit the profile since he is not an English native speaker and not based in the right time zone,

Andy Dustman

Dustman's email address is from the University of Georgia, and he only contributed 11 posts. His LinkedIn page (`www.linkedin.com/in/andydustman/`) indicates that he is American, studied chemistry from 1987 to 1991 and 1995 to 1997, and was based in Georgia until 2014. He is a Python and database programmer with no record of programming in C++. He does not fit the profile for location and language and is slightly older.

Bill Frantz

Bill Frantz was quite active with more than 200 comments. The listed email is from an American Internet provider (Netcom). He seems later to be critical of Bitcoin in a recent post from 2021 (`www.metzdowd.com/pipermail/cryptography/2021-January/036533.html`). The email and signature indicate he is working at PwC and lives in New Hampshire. Frantz seems to have specialized in financial cryptography as can be seen from his ResearchGate profile (`www.researchgate.net/profile/Bill-Frantz`). He also published together with among others Ron Rivest on this topic:

Carl M. Ellison, Bill Frantz, Butler W. Lampson, Ron Rivest, Brian Thomas, Tatu Ylönen:

SPKI Certificate Theory. RFC 2693: 1–43 (1999)

Capability-Based Financial Instruments. Financial Cryptography 2000: 349–378

Although he seems to be capable in many of the disciplines involved in the creation of Bitcoin, he seems significantly older than the profile based on pictures. He is also American and there is no evidence he is able to code in C++.

Duncan Frissell

Duncan Frissell has an email address from `https://panix.com`, which is a New York–based Internet provider. There is one Duncan Frissell on LinkedIn (`www.linkedin.com/in/duncan-frissell-32498646/`). He worked for the Port Authority of New York and New Jersey for 31 years and is retired now. Frisell studied economics and law from 1969 to 1976. He does not match the age of the profile, and there is no evidence that he was able to code.

Jim Choate

Jim Choate was very active with more than 800 posts on the cryptography mailing list. In fact, he was the one who set up the cypherpunk mailing list according to the Wikipedia article on cypherpunks. Earlier he used an email address from bga.com, which at the time was the Texas-based Real Time Communications company, an Internet provider. Another site ssz.com seems to be based in Texas. He was therefore probably based in Texas working with mail and Internet infrastructure services. He seems focused more on free speech than virtual currencies, and not much else can be said.

Mark Fisher

Mark Fisher's email is from cyberpass.net, but he also has another email address on the mailing list with a signature that indicates he worked for Thomson Consumer Electronics in Indianapolis in 1997. I found one publication on ResearchGate that he wrote while working for Thomson in 1997 called "The TCE Corporate Technical Memory: groupware on the cheap." I also found him on GitHub: `https://github.com/markleightonfisher`. According to his GitHub repository, he programs mainly in Ruby and PERL and not in C++. His LinkedIn profile (`www.linkedin.com/in/mark-leighton-fisher/`) indicates he worked at Thomson Consumer Electronics from 1991 to 2003. According to that, however, he does know C++.

In the previous work experience, he writes that he works primarily in C and less in C++. He has been based in Indiana from 2005 working at Regenstrief Institute and was educated at Purdue in electrical engineering from 1975 to 1980. He does not match the profile for age, location, and nationality but seems to know C++.

Ian Grigg

Ian Grigg has an email address from Systemics, which is a company that worked with digital payment in the financial cryptography area. Their website still exists, but they seem not to be active since 2001. Grigg was the author of the triple-entry accounting paper that was mentioned in Chapter 3. He developed his own virtual currency, DigiGold, in 1999, which was a competitor to Bitcoin. He was probably born before 1970 to judge from publications and age on pictures. He does not match the age of the profile and is American, and it is strange that he would also publicly be promoting a competitor to Bitcoin if he was the author of it.

Dave Birch

Dave Birch only wrote three posts. All of them seem to be about virtual currencies though. But he seems to be against the cypherpunk idea of electronic cash. His response to Dai is that instead of a basket of commodities, the value could be tied to future services like frequent flyer miles. His company's website indicates that he is based in the United Kingdom as can be seen from a snapshot from 1997 (https://web. archive.org/web/19970213190218/http://www.hyperion.co.uk/). The company has public addresses in the United Kingdom, Surrey, and Scotland. It was started in the mid-1980s by Logika Consultants. Dave Birch was among them. In 1989 he and two others bought out the others and grew the company. This means that Dave Birch was a consultant who must have studied at the latest in the early 1980s, which means that he does not match the age profile of Satoshi. I found his web page: www.dgwbirch.com/biography/consult-hyperion.html.

He is the author of three books. One is also about Bitcoin. Although Birch is British and based in the United Kingdom, the age does not match, and there is no indication that he has the technical skills either.

Bibliography

Introduction

Satoshi Nakamoto, 2008, *Bitcoin: A Peer-to-Peer Electronic Cash System* (https://bitcoin.org/bitcoin.pdf)

Timothy Morton, 2014, *Hyperobjects: Philosophy and Ecology After the End of the World*, University of Minnesota Press

Michel Foucault, 1984, "Of other spaces: utopias and heterotopias," Architecture /Mouvement/ Continuité

Finn Brunton, 2019, *Digital Cash: The Unknown History of the Anarchists, Utopians, and Technologists Who Created Cryptocurrency*, Princeton University Press

Phil Champagne, 2014, *The Book of Satoshi*, Wren Investment Group LLC

Chapter 1

Niall Ferguson, 2009, *The Ascent of Money: A Financial History of the World: 10th Anniversary Edition*, Penguin

European Central Bank, 2012, "Virtual Currency Schemes" (www.ecb.europa.eu/pub/pdf/other/virtualcurrencyschemes201210en.pdf)

European Central Bank, 2018, "Crypto-Assets: Implications for financial stability, monetary policy, and payments and market infrastructures" (www.ecb.europa.eu/pub/pdf/scpops/ecb.op223~3ce14e986c.en.pdf)

Department of the Treasury, 2013, "Financial Crimes Enforcement Network: Application of FinCEN's Regulations to Persons Administering, Exchanging, or Using Virtual Currencies" (www.fincen.gov/resources/statutes-regulations/guidance/application-fincens-regulations-persons-administering)

Steven Horwitz, 2020, *Austrian Economics: An Introduction*, Cato Institute

Vernor Vinge, 1981, *True Names*, Dell Publishing

William Gibson, 1984, *Neuromancer*, Ace

Neal Stephenson, 1992, *Snow Crash*, Bantam Books

Timothy C. May, 1982, *The Crypto Anarchist Manifesto*

David Chaum, "Blind signatures for untraceable payments" (https://sceweb.sce.uhcl.edu/yang/teaching/csci5234WebSecurity Fall2011/Chaum-blind-signatures.pdf)

Saifedean Ammous, 2018, *The Bitcoin Standard: The Decentralized Alternative to Central Banking*, Wiley

Kim Zetter, June 8, 2009, "Bullion and Bandits," Wired

Lawrence H. White, 2014, "The Troubling Suppression of Competition from Alternative Monies: The Cases of the Liberty Dollar and E-Gold," Cato Journal

Conor Grant, 2018, "A decade before crypto, one digital currency conquered the world—then failed spectacularly" (https://thehustle.co/beenz-pre-bitcoin-digital-currency/)

Maya Kosoff, October 2016, "These dot-com startups look just like some of today's hottest tech companies—here's what happened to them," Business Insider

Adam Back, 2002, "Hashcash—a denial of service counter-measure" (www.hashcash.org/papers/hashcash.pdf)

Wei Dai, 1997, "B-money" (www.weidai.com/bmoney.txt)

Chapter 2

Simon Singh, 1999, *The Code Book: The Science of Secrecy from Ancient Egypt to Quantum Cryptography*, Fourth Estate and Doubleday

Whitfield Diffe and Martin E. Hellman, 1976, "New Directions in Cryptography," IEEE Transactions on Information Theory

R. L. Rivest, A. Shamir, and L. Adleman, 1978, "A Method for Obtaining Digital Signatures and Public-Key Cryptosystems," Communications of the ACM, Volume 21, Issue 2, pp. 120–126

Cynthia Dwork and Moni Naor, 1993, "Pricing via processing or combatting Junk mail," in *Advances in Cryptology—CRYPTO' 92* (ed. Brickell, E. F.), Lecture Notes in Computer Science, Volume 740, Springer

Markus Jakobson and Ari Juuls, 1999, "Proofs of work and bread pudding protocols," in *Secure Information Networks: Communications and Multimedia Security* (ed. Preneel, B.), Springer Verlag

Bart Preneel, 2010, "The First 30 Years of Cryptographic Hash Functions and the NIST SHA-3 Competition," in *Topics in Cryptology—CT-RSA 2010, The Cryptographers' Track at the RSA Conference* (ed. Pieprzyk, J.), Lecture Notes in Computer Science, Volume 5985, pp. 1–14, Springer Verlag

Ronald Rivest and Adi Shamir, 2005, "PayWord and MicroMint: Two simple micropayment schemes," Lecture Notes in Computer Science, Volume 1189

Chapter 3

Glyn Davies, 2016, *A History of Money*, University of Wales Press

Yuji Ijiri, "Triple-Entry Bookkeeping and Income Momentum," American Accounting Association

Ian Grigg, 2005, "Tripple entry accounting," working paper (https://iang.org/papers/triple_entry.html)

Edgar F. Codd, 2000, *The Relational Model for Database Management*, Addison-Wesley

Stuart Haber and Wakefield Stornetta, 1990, "How to time-stamp a digital document," Journal of Cryptology

Samuel Haig, "Legendary Cryptographer on Building the First Blockchain in the '90s," Cointelegraph (`https://cointelegraph.com/news/legendary-cryptographer-on-building-the-first-blockchain-in-the-90s`)

Chapter 4

Anthony Lewis, 2018, *The Basics of Bitcoins and Blockchains: An Introduction to Cryptocurrencies and the Technology that Powers Them*, Mango

Andreas M. Antonopoulos, 2017, *Mastering Bitcoin: Programming the Open Blockchain*, O'Reilly Media

Chapter 5

Joshua Davis, 2011, "The crypto-currency," New Yorker

Adam L. Penenberg, 2011, "The Bitcoin Crypto-Currency Mystery Reopened," Fast Company

Ted Nelson, 2013, "I Think I Know Who Satoshi Is," YouTube (`www.youtube.com/watch?v=emDJTGTrEmO`)

Alec Liu, "Who Is Satoshi Nakamoto, the Creator of Bitcoin?", vice.com

Leah McGrath Goodman, 2014, "The Face Behind Bitcoin," Newsweek

Andy Greenberg, 2014, "Nakamoto's Neighbor: My Hunt For Bitcoin's Creator Led To A Paralyzed Crypto Genius," Forbes

John Biggs, 2014, "Who is the real Satoshi Nakamoto? One researcher may have found the answer," TechCrunch

Skye Grey, 2013, "Satoshi Nakamoto is (probably) Nick Szabo" (`https://likeinamirror.wordpress.com/2013/12/01/satoshi-nakamoto-is-probably-nick-szabo/`)

Rob Wile, 2014, "The Hunt For The Creator Of Bitcoin Keeps Coming Back To One Guy—And He May Be Hiding In Plain Sight," Business Insider

Rob Wile, 2014, "PROFESSOR: There Is A Big, Gaping Flaw In The New Satoshi Study," Business Insider

Dominic Frisby, 2014, *Bitcoin: The Future of Money?*, Unbound

Nathaniel Popper, 2015, "Digital Gold," Harper Paperbacks

Chapter 6

Georg G. Iggers, 2005, *Historiography in the Twentieth Century: From Scientific Objectivity to the Postmodern Challenge*, Wesleyan University Press

Original announcement of Bitcoin: `www.metzdowd.com/pipermail/cryptography/2008-October/014810.html`

Original Bitcoin whitepaper: `https://bitcoin.org/bitcoin.pdf`

Forum posts: `https://satoshi.nakamotoinstitute.org/posts/`

Cypherpunk mailing list: `https://mailing-list-archive.cryptoanarchy.wiki/`

Cryptography mailing list: `www.metzdowd.com/pipermail/cryptography/`

Jamie Redman, 2020, "New Research Suggests Satoshi Nakamoto Lived in London Creating Bitcoin," Bitcoin.com (`https://news.bitcoin.com/new-research-suggests-satoshi-nakamoto-lived-in-london-creating-bitcoin/`)

Doncho Karaivanov, 2020, "Satoshi Nakamoto Lived in London While Working on Bitcoin. Here's How We Know," The Chain Bulletin (`https://chainbulletin.com/satoshi-nakamoto-lived-in-london-while-working-on-bitcoin-heres-how-we-know`)

Wei Dai/Satoshi Nakamoto, 2009, Bitcoin emails: `https://gwern.net/doc/bitcoin/2008-nakamoto`

Barely Sociable, "Bitcoin—Unmasking Satoshi Nakamoto" (`www.youtube.com/watch?v=XfcvXOP1b5g&t=2103s`)

Chapter 7

Adam Back's homepage: `www.cypherspace.org/adam/`

Adam Back's LinkedIn page: `www.linkedin.com/in/adam-back-043342/`

Bitcoin Talk: `https://bitcointalk.org`

Adam Back's introduction on Bitcoin Talk: `https://bitcointalk.org/index.php?topic=225463.0`

Back claims to have communicated but refuses to share them. He may have deleted the emails: `https://cointelegraph.com/news/adam-back-on-satoshi-emails-privacy-concerns-and-bitcoins-early-days`

Adam Back in 1997 proposed the following as a substitution for DigiCash: `https://mailing-list-archive.cryptoanarchy.wiki/archive/1997/04/cd7308e7335eccf7d361a1bdbe32736f9ee965d80c0c3cfaca8f2d363aeb6312/`

In this post he proposes Hashcash. The cryptographic requirements for a system such as this would be

1) Being anonymous (privacy preserving, payee and payer anonymous

2) Being distributed (to make it hard to shut down)

3) Having some built-in scarcity

4) Requiring no trust of any one individual

5) Preferably being offline (difficult to do with pure software)

6) Being reusable

It seems that already in 1999 someone anonymous replying to a thread on ecash by Adam Back pointed out ideas that are similar to the later Bitcoin whitepaper. It also cites Wei Dai and Adam Back's Hashcash: https://marc.info/?l=cypherpunks&m=95280154629912&w=2

Could this anonymous person be Satoshi as Adam Back himself suggests on May 14, 2013?: https://bitcointalk.org/index.php?action=profile;threads;u=101601;sa=showPosts;start=20 https://bitcointalk.org/index.php?action=profile;threads;u=101601;sa=showPosts;start=20

Chapter 8

Glyn Davies, 2016, *A History of Money*, University of Wales Press

John Liep, 2009, *A Papuan Plutocracy: Ranked Exchange on Rossel Island*, Aarhus Universitetsforlag

Chuck Sudetic, 1093, "Cigarettes a Thriving Industry in Bleak Sarajevo," The New York Times

Saskatchewan newspaper in January 5, 1946 (https://news.google.com/newspapers?id=YL9TAAAAIBAJ&sjid=gzgNAAAAIBAJ&pg=553 5%2C527446)

"What do British prisoners use as currency?", The Guardian, 2016 (www.theguardian.com/society/shortcuts/2016/aug/23/what-do-british-prisoners-use-as-currency)

Wim Hordijk, 2014, "From Salt To Salary: Linguists Take A Page From Science," npr.org

William S. Jevons, 1989, "Money and the Mechanism of Exchange," in *General Equilibrium Models of Monetary Economies*, pp. 55–65, Academic Press

Michael Tomasello, 2018, *A Natural History of Human Thinking*, Harvard University Press

Marcel Mauss, 2000, *The Gift: The Form and Reason for Exchange in Archaic Societies*, WW Norton & Company

Bronislaw Malinowski, 2013, *Argonauts of the Western Pacific: An Account of Native Enterprise and Adventure in the Archipelagoes of Melanesian New Guinea*, Routledge

Philip Grierson, 1977, *The Origins of Money*, The Athlone Press of the University of London

Paul Einzig, 2014, *Primitive Money in Its Ethnological, Historical and Economic Aspects*, Elsevier

David Graeber, 2012, *Debt: The First 5000 Years*, Penguin UK

Saifedean Ammous, 2018, *The Bitcoin Standard: The Decentralized Alternative to Central Banking*, Wiley

Chapter 9

Steven Levy, 1984, *Hackers: Heroes of the Computer Revolution*, Anchor Press/Doubleday

Walter Isaacson, 2011, *Steve Jobs*, Simon & Schuster

Nadia Eghbal, *Working in Public: The Making and Maintenance of Open Source Software*, Stripe Press

David Chaum, 1985, "Security without identification: transaction systems to make big brother obsolete," Communications of the ACM, Volume 28, Issue 10, 1030–1044

Mary Douglas, 2003, *Natural Symbols*, Routledge Classics

Chapter 10

Quotes are from the question on Quora "When will cryptocurrency holders realize that cryptocurrency is a scam?" (www.quora.com/When-will-cryptocurrency-holders-realize-that-cryptocurrency-is-a-scam)

Armin W. Geertz, 1999, "Definition as analytical strategy in the study of religion," Historical Reflections/Reflexions Historiques, 445–475

Niels Peter Lemche, *The Israelites in History and Tradition*, Westminster John Knox Press

Edward Conze, 2014, *Buddhist Texts Through the Ages*, Open Road Media

Peter Worsley, *The Trumpet Shall Sound: A Study of Cargo Cults in Melanesia*," London MacGibbon & Kee

Ray Kurzweil, 2000, *The Age of Spiritual Machines*, Penguin

Meghan O'Gieblyn, 2021, *God, Human, Animal, Machine: Technology, Metaphor, and the Search for Meaning*, Anchor

Julian Huxley, 1951, "Knowledge, morality, and destiny: I," Psychiatry, Volume 14, Issue 2, 129–140

Pierre Teilhard de Chardin, 1947, "The formation of the noosphere, the future of man," Doubleday New York

Peter Harrison and Joseph Wolyniak, 2015, "History of transhumanism," Notes and Queries, Volume 62, Issue 3, 465–467

Finn Brunton, 2019, *Digital Cash: The Unknown History of the Anarchists, Utopians, and Technologists Who Created Cryptocurrency*, Princeton University Press

David Chaum, "Blinding for Unanticipated Signatures," in *Advances in Cryptology—EUROCRYPT '87* (eds Chaum, D. & Price, W. L.), pp. 227–233, Springer Verlag

Chapter 11

Alun John, Samuel Shen, and Tom Wilson, September 24, 2021, "China's top regulators ban crypto trading and mining, sending bitcoin tumbling," Reuters

Mogens Herman Hansen (ed.), 2000, "A comparative study of thirty city-state cultures: an investigation," Kgl. Danske Videnskabernes Selskab

Cassandra C. Wang, Julie T. Miao, Nicholas A. Phelps, and Jia Zhang, 2021, "E-commerce and the transformation of the rural: the Taobao village phenomenon in Zhejiang Province, China," Journal of Rural Studies, Volume 81, 159–169

Ray Kurzweil, 2005, *The Singularity Is Near: When Humans Transcend Biology*, Penguin

Nick Bostrom, 2014, *Superintelligence: Paths, Dangers, Strategies*, Oxford University Press

Max Tegmark, 2017, *Life 3.0*, Penguin

David Chalmers, 2014, "Mind Uploading: A Philosophical Analysis," in *Intelligence Unbound: The Future of Uploaded and Machine Minds* (eds Blackford, R. and Broderick, D.), Wiley-Blackwell

Leonard David, 2015, "Lunar Lava Tubes Might Make Underground Moon Cities Possible," Space Insider

Adam Becker, 2015, "Space scientists are pouring much time and effort into colonising Mars. But could we also live in the atmosphere of Venus? BBC Future investigates," bbc.com

Chapter 12

Timothy Morton, 2014, *Hyperobjects: Philosophy and Ecology After the End of the World*, University of Minnesota Press

Corey S. Powell, September 7, 2019, "Strange life forms found deep in a mine point to vast underground Galapagos," NBC News

Erwin Schrödinger, *What Is Life? With Mind and Matter and Autobiographical Sketches*, Cambridge University Press

Humberto R. Maturana and Francisco J. Varela, 1991, *Autopoiesis and Cognition: The Realization of the Living*, Springer Science & Business Media, Volume 42

Merlin Sheldrake, 2020, *Entangled Life: How Fungi Make Our Worlds, Change Our Minds & Shape Our Futures*, Random House

Richard Dawkins, 1976, *The Selfish Gene*, Oxford University Press

Index

© Anders Lisdorf 2023
A. Lisdorf, *Still Searching for Satoshi*, https://doi.org/10.1007/978-1-4842-9639-4

Printed in the United States
by Baker & Taylor Publisher Services